Coding as a

Coding as a Playground is the first book to focus on how young children (ages 7 and under) can engage in computational thinking and be taught to become computer programmers, a process that can increase both their cognitive and social-emotional skills. Readers will learn how coding can engage children as producers—and not merely consumers—of technology in a playful way. You will come away from this groundbreaking work with an understanding of how coding promotes developmentally appropriate experiences such as problem solving, imagination, cognitive challenges, social interactions, motor skills development, emotional exploration, and making different choices. You will also learn how to integrate coding into different curricular areas to promote literacy, math, science, engineering, and the arts through a project-based approach.

Marina Umaschi Bers is a professor in the Eliot-Pearson Department of Child Study and Human Development and an adjunct professor in the Computer Science Department at Tufts University. She heads the Developmental Technologies Research group where she studies innovative ways to promote positive childhood development through new learning technologies. Marina co-developed the ScratchJr programming language in collaboration with Mitch Resnick from the MIT Media Lab and Paula Bonta from the PICO company. She is also the creator of KIBO, a robotics platform for children 4 to 7 that can be programmed with wooden blocks (no screen needed), which allows young builders to learn programming and engineering while integrating arts and crafts.

Coding as a Playground

Programming and Computational Thinking in the Early Childhood Classroom

Marina Umaschi Bers

Routledge
Taylor & Francis Group

NEW YORK AND LONDON

First published 2018
by Routledge
711 Third Avenue, New York, NY 10017

and by Routledge
2 Park Square, Milton Park, Abingdon, Oxon, OX14 4RN

Routledge is an imprint of the Taylor & Francis Group, an informa business

Library of Congress Cataloging-in-Publication Data
A catalog record for this book has been requested

ISBN: 978-1-138-22561-9 (hbk)
ISBN: 978-1-138-22562-6 (pbk)
ISBN: 978-1-315-39894-5 (ebk)

Typeset in Optima
by Apex CoVantage, LLC

Contents

Meet the Author

Marina Umaschi Bers was born in Argentina and moved to the U.S. in 1994 for grad school. She received a Master's degree in Educational Media from Boston University and an MS and PhD from the MIT Media Laboratory, where she worked with Seymour Papert. Today, she is a professor at the Eliot-Pearson Department of Child Study and Human Development and the Computer Science Department at Tufts University, and she heads the interdisciplinary DevTech research group. Her research involves the design and study of innovative learning technologies to promote positive youth development.

Dr. Bers was awarded the prestigious 2005 Presidential Early Career Award for Scientists and Engineers (PECASE), an NSF Career Award, and the American Educational Research Association's Jan Hawkins Award. Over the past 20 years, she has conceived, designed, and evaluated diverse educational technologies ranging from robotics to virtual worlds. When she had her own three children, Tali, Alan and Nico, she decided to focus her research on technological environments for young children, 4 to 7 years old. Dr. Bers has received multiple grants that allowed her to develop and research such technologies, resulting in ScratchJr, a free programming app, and KIBO, a robotics kit that can be programmed with wooden blocks, sold by KinderLab Robotics, Inc. (a company she co-founded in 2013 and for which she received the 2015 Women to Watch award by the *Boston Business Journal*).

Dr. Bers' philosophy and theoretical approach for developing these technologies, as well as her pedagogical approach, curriculum, and assessment methods, can be found in her books *Blocks to Robots: Learning With Technology in the Early Childhood Classroom* (2008; Teacher's College Press), *Designing Digital Experiences for Positive Youth Development: From*

Playpen to Playground (2012, Oxford University Press), and most recently *The Official ScratchJr Book* (2015; No Starch Press). Dr. Bers loves teaching, and in 2016 she received the Outstanding Faculty Contribution to Graduate Student Studies award at Tufts University. In addition, she teaches seminars on learning technologies for educators and does extensive consulting for schools, museums, after school settings, toy and media companies and non profits.

More on Dr. Bers: www.tufts.edu/~mbers01/

Acknowledgments

"Much have I learned from my teachers, more from my colleagues, but most from my students" (Talmud, Ta'anit 7b). This book is the result of many years of conversations and explorations, collaborations, and observations. My journey into coding began in the mid-1970s, back in my homeland of Buenos Aires, Argentina. I was only 8 years old when my parents signed me up for a computer programming class to learn LOGO. Little did I know that decades later Seymour Papert, the father of LOGO, was going to become my mentor. Throughout my doctoral work at the MIT Media Lab, Seymour guided me to find good questions to ask and pushed me to pursue my dreams and ambitions. Mitch Resnick, a young professor at the time, provided me with the needed steady support. Years later, it is an honor and a privilege to collaborate with him on projects such as ScratchJr and discuss ideas over breakfast, eating his homemade bread. Sherry Turkle, my doctoral thesis reader and always present inspiration, still reminds me about the importance of bringing humanity back to technology.

While at MIT, I mostly conducted research with programming languages and educational robotics with elementary and high school children. However, when I had my own children and became a young assistant professor at Tufts University, I quickly realized the need for bringing ideas from computer science to the early years. My colleagues at the Eliot Pearson Department of Child Study and Human Development became my teachers. In particular, Debbie LeeKennan, who was then the director of the Eliot Pearson Children's School, Becky New, then director of the Early Childhood Education Program, David Elkind, David Henry Feldman, and Richard Lerner. Chris Rogers, professor of Mechanical Engineering and founder of the Center for Engineering Education and Outreach at Tufts, became a "partner in crime," always ready to go on a walk to discuss co-teaching a course, to design educational toys, maker spaces, 3D printing, or simply providing wise advice.

I was always fascinated with the similarities between written and programming languages, and with the potential of coding to become a literacy that can truly impact the way we think and bring about educational and societal change. For writing this book, I went back to readings I had done on the topic of literacy and orality when I was doing my undergraduate studies and working as a teaching assistant with Anibal Ford and Alejandro Piscitelli at the Universidad de Buenos Aires. This time, I read those old books and articles with a different lens. I felt that the circle was closing. I started my academic life looking at the role of language and stories, communication and expression. Now, 22 years later, I came back to those seminal ideas.

Over the years, I have been privileged to have an amazing interdisciplinary group of undergraduate and graduate students, as well as research staff, working on my DevTech research group at Tufts University. Amanda Strawhacker and Kaitlyn Leidl have directly contributed to some of the research and vignettes presented in this book on ScratchJr. Amanda Sullivan has become my right hand at the lab, participated in all the research work on KIBO, contributed with literature reviews and vignettes, and conducted a thorough editing of this book. I am indebted to her, not only for her intellectual contributions to the research, but for her kindness and good spirits. When KIBO became ready to leave Tufts University and become a product, Mitch Rosenberg and I initiated a life-transforming adventure of co-founding KinderLab Robotics to commercialize KIBO and take it worldwide. I thank him for believing in my ideas and putting his heart and soul into this journey.

I wrote this book in our new home on the lake. It is the beginning of a new time in my life. The sun is bright and the water is peaceful. I deeply want to thank my husband, Pato O'Donnell, for so much love, caring, and everything else. Wholeness came to my life. My three children, Tali, Alan, and Nico, are my life teachers and my harshest critics when designing programming environments. Gracias, chicos, por todo! My mother, Lydia, had the early vision to introduce me to computer programming and is a constant fan and supporter. I couldn't work and be the mother that I am without her help. My dad passed away too young, but there are sparks of him in everything I do.

I thank the National Science Foundation for supporting my work and the people who read early drafts of this book and gave me valuable feedback: Amanda Sullivan, Amanda Strawhacker, Paula Bonta, Cynthia Solomon, Adeline Yeo, Claudia Mihm, and Clara Hill. Finally, I want to thank the thousands of children and early childhood educators, principals, and administrators, all over the world, who have been part of my research over so many years. I have learned from them what no book can teach us.

Introduction

Liana, 5 years old, is sitting with an iPad in her kindergarten class. She is focused. Every so often, she wiggles. She suddenly screams, to no one in particular, "Look at my cat! Look at my cat!" Liana is excited to show her animation. She has programmed the ScratchJr kitten to appear and disappear on the screen ten different times. She has put together a long sequence of graphical programming blocks, purple blocks to be more specific, called Looks blocks. Liana cannot read yet, but she just knows that these programming blocks can make her ScratchJr kitten show and hide. She is in control of the kitten's behaviors. She can decide how many times it will appear and disappear on the screen by choosing the blocks to put together in a sequence. As a 5-year-old, Liana, like most children her age, wants to make the longest possible sequence, so she puts together a script with ten blocks, until she runs out of space in the programming area.

When Liana's kindergarten teacher hears her excitement, she walks over to see Liana's project. Liana is proud to show "my movie," as she calls it. "I made it. Look at my cat. It appears and disappears, it appears and disappears, it appears and disappears. Many times. Look!" She clicks on the green flag on the ScratchJr interface and the animation starts. At that point, Liana's teacher asks her, "How many times does the kitten show and hide?" "Ten times," replies Liana. "I ran out of room. I wanted more times." The teacher shows her a long orange programming block, called "Repeat." This block allows for other blocks to be inserted inside its "loop." It then runs the blocks inside the loop as many times as the programmer decides. Liana notices that this block looks slightly different than the purple ones and it is orange. It belongs to a different category, called "Control Blocks."

After some trial and error, in which Liana plays with inserting different combinations of the show and hide purple blocks inside the repeat block, she figures it out. She can put just one of each purple block inside the repeat block, and set the number of repetition times to the highest she can think of. She chooses the number 99 and clicks the green flag to see the animation. The kitten starts appearing and disappearing. After a few seconds, she gets bored of watching. So she goes back to her code and changes the number of repetitions to 20 (see Figure 0.1).

During this experience, Liana engaged with some of the most power-ful ideas of computer sciences that are accessible for a young child. She also developed computational thinking. She learned that a programing lan-guage has a syntax in which symbols represent actions. She understood that her choices had an impact on what was happening on the screen. She was able to create a sequence of programming blocks to represent a complex behavior (e.g., appearing and disappearing). She used logic in a systematic way to correctly order the blocks in a sequence. She practiced and applied the concept of patterns, which she had learned earlier in the year during math time in class. She learned new blocks that allowed her to achieve her goals. She discovered the concept of loops and parameters. At the same time, she engaged in problem solving and also exercised her

Figure 0.1 The ScratchJr interface with Liana's "Disappearing Kitten" program. In this photo, the kitten is programmed with a repeat loop to appear and disappear 20 times.

tenacity at tackling something she truly cared about (i.e., having a very long kitten movie). Finally, Liana was able to create a project from her own original idea and turn it into a final product, a project she chose and to which she was personally attached. She was proud to share it with others and happy to revise it when the final outcome did not meet her expectations (i.e., it ended up being so long that it was boring to watch). She also engaged with mathematical ideas of estimation and number sense (i.e., 99 is way longer than 20).

To code, Liana used ScratchJr, a programming language specifically designed for young children that runs on tablets as well as desktops, and that can be downloaded for free. ScratchJr was designed and developed by my DevTech research group at Tufts University in collaboration with Mitch Resnick's Lifelong Kindergarten group at the MIT Media Lab and Paula Bonta and Brian Silverman from the PICO company in Canada. To date, over 6 million young children all over the world are using ScratchJr to create their own projects.

Liana's teacher integrated ScratchJr in a learning environment in which children had the freedom to make a project they cared about. Liana was excited and passionate. She was not going to give up until her cat did exactly what she wanted. She worked hard and she rejoiced in that process. She enjoyed learning and was fully engaged in it. For her, developing computational thinking involved more than problem solving; it meant gaining the concepts, skills, and habits of mind to express herself through coding.

This book explores the role of coding for young children. Most specifically, it focuses on the developmental milestones and learning experiences that children can attain by becoming programmers and by thinking like computer scientists. Coding engages children as producers, and not merely consumers, of technology. Children such as Liana can create their own movies or animations, interactive games or stories. Coding is not only a cognitive activity that involves problem solving and mastering programming concepts and skills, but also an expressive medium that engages emotional and social domains. Liana stuck to her project and debugged it because she truly cared about it. She felt proud and in control. Her "cat movie" allowed her to show an aspect of who she is. Liana loves animated movies and she was thrilled to make her own.

Just like any natural language—English, Spanish, or Japanese—that allows us to express our needs and desires, our discoveries and frustrations, our dreams and everyday doings, programming languages such as ScratchJr provide a tool for expression. We need to learn their syntax and grammars and, over time, the more we engage with them, the more fluent we become. We know when we have truly learned a new language because we are able to use it for different purposes: to write a love poem, to make a shopping list for the supermarket, to compose an academic essay, to order a pizza, or to discuss political events at a social gathering. A language helps us think and communicate in new ways. Furthermore, the night we dream in that new language, we know we have mastered it.

Coding With Objects

Programming languages have different interfaces that support different ways of expression. Coding can happen on the screen, as in Liana's case with ScratchJr, or it can happen through objects in the world. For example, the KIBO robot, also developed in my DevTech research lab at Tufts University and now commercialized by KinderLab Robotics, allows young children to code without screens of any kind. The programming language is composed of wooden blocks with pegs and holes that can be inserted into each other forming a tangible sequence of commands. Each block represents an instruction for KIBO: forward, shake, wait for clap, light on, beep, etc.

Let's look at Maya and Natan's experience with KIBO. They are also in kindergarten. They are working on a joint KIBO robotics project. Maya is choosing the blocks to make KIBO dance the Hokey Pokey. She starts with the green "begin" block and concludes with the red "end" block. She needs to figure out the blocks in between. She forgot the KIBO Hokey Pokey song the teacher taught them, so she is at loss about what blocks to choose. Natan, her teammate, reminds her of the song:

> You put your robot in
> You put your robot out
> You put your robot in
> And you shake it all about
> You do the Hokey Pokey
> and you turn yourself around
> That's what it's all about!

Maya sings along and, as the song progresses, she chooses the blocks and starts putting them together in a sequence. Begin; "You put your robot in," forward; "You put your robot out," backward; "You put your robot in," forward; "And you shake it all about." She suddenly stops and says, "Natan, I can't find the 'do the Hokey Pokey' block!" "There is no block for that, silly," responds Natan. "We need to make it up. Let's have KIBO turn on the blue and red light instead. That will be our Hokey Pokey block." Maya agrees, adds those two blocks to the sequence and also adds "shake," "spin," and "beep" to represent the "what it's all about" part of the song. Maya and Natan look at their program while singing the song to make sure they have put together all the needed blocks. Then they turn on KIBO to test things out. The red light of KIBO's scanner (the "mouth," as Maya calls it) is flashing, meaning that the robot is ready to scan each of the barcodes printed on the wooden programming blocks (see Figure 0.2).

Natan takes his turn and scans the blocks one by one. He goes too fast and skips the "red light" block. Maya points that out, and he restarts the scanning. The children are excited to see their robot dance the Hokey

Figure 0.2 The KIBO robot scanning a version of the HokeyPokey Program: Begin, forward, backward, forward, shake, spin, end.

Pokey. "When I count to three, you start singing," says Maya to Natan. They know the drill. They have practiced it during technology circle time in class. Natan sings and both KIBO and Maya dance the Hokey Pokey. It goes too fast. KIBO dances too fast. "Can you sing faster?" asks Maya. Natan tries one more time, but it still doesn't work. "We have a problem." he says. "I can't sing fast enough to keep up with KIBO." Maya has an idea. For each action in the song she puts two blocks, so KIBO's motions will last longer. For example, for the "you put your robot in" part, instead of just one "forward" block, she puts two forwards, and so on for each of the commands. Natan tries singing again, and this time KIBO dances at the same pace.

Both children start clapping, shaking their bodies, and jumping up and down. Without knowing it, just like Liana with her ScratchJr animation, they engaged with many powerful ideas of computer science, such as sequencing, algorithmic thinking, and problem solving. They also explored math concepts they are learning in kindergarten, such as estimation, prediction, and counting. Furthermore, they engaged in collaboration. "Children already have too much screen time at home. When they are at school I want them learning new concepts and skills in STEM, but as importantly, I want them learning to socialize and collaborate with others. I want them looking at each other, and not at the screen," explains Marisa, their kindergarten teacher. "KIBO is just perfect for that."

During technology circle time, Marisa asks every group of children to give a demo of their dancing KIBOs. Everyone else is invited to stand up and dance alongside. There is laughter and clapping. There is physical activity, socialization, language development, problem solving, and creative play. It is fun. It feels like a playground, not a coding class. In previous work, I coined the metaphor "playground vs. playpen" (Bers, 2012) to discuss the role that new technologies can have in young children's lives. Coding can become a playground, an environment to be creative, to express ourselves, to explore alone and with others, to learn new skills, and to problem solve. All of this, while having fun.

High-Tech Playgrounds

Playgrounds are open-ended. Playpens are limited. Playgrounds invite fantasy play, imagination, and creativity. The "playground vs. playpen" metaphor provides a way to understand the kind of developmentally appropriate experiences that new technologies, such as programming languages, can promote: problem solving, imagination, cognitive challenges, social interactions, motor skills development, emotional exploration, and making different choices. In contrast to the open-ended playground, playpens convey lack of freedom to experiment, lack of autonomy for exploration, lack of creative opportunities, and lack of taking risks. Although playpens are safer, playgrounds provide infinite possibilities for growth and learning.

This book focuses on the activity of coding as a playground. Coding can happen by using different programing languages, just as expressing ourselves can happen through different natural languages such as Spanish, English, or Mandarin. Liana used ScratchJr to make an animated movie of her kitten appearing and disappearing. Maya and Natan used KIBO's wooden blocks to make the robot dance the Hokey Pokey. They all became programmers, producers, makers of their own projects. Throughout the book, we will learn more about both ScratchJr and KIBO. We will also explore the potential of powerful ideas of computer science for early childhood education. In this book I am proposing a playful approach: a playground approach, and not a playpen approach. In this journey, we will also dive into the role of computational thinking and its relationship to coding.

Coding in Early Childhood

There is a new push for coding. President Obama became the first U.S. president to write a line of code during a very publicized event. His administration launched the Computer Science for All initiative, which hopes to bring programming into every single educational level (Smith, 2016). Research and policy changes over the recent years have brought a new-found focus to coding (Sesame Workshop, 2009; Barron et al., 2011; International Society for Technology in Education (ISTE), 2007; NAEYC and Fred Rogers Center for Early Learning and Children's Media, 2012; U.S. Department of Education, 2010; A framework for K12 CS, https://k12cs.org/). As of the writing of this book, 16 countries in Europe alone integrate coding into the curriculum at the national, regional, or local level, including: Austria, Bulgaria, the Czech Republic, Denmark, Estonia, France, Hungary, Ireland, Israel, Lithuania, Malta, Spain, Poland, Portugal, Slovakia, and the UK (Balanskat & Engelhardt, 2015; European Schoolnet, 2014;

Livingstone, 2012). Outside of Europe, countries such as Australia and Singapore have also established clear policies and frameworks for introducing technology and computer programming in K12 education (Australian Curriculum Assessment and Reporting Authority, 2015; Digital News Asia, 2015; Siu & Lam, 2003). When compared with other countries, the U.S. lags behind, with only one in four schools teaching computer science, and only 32 states allowing computer science courses to count toward high school graduation. Of those states, only seven currently have computer science curriculum standards in grades K12 (Code.org, 2016).

Regardless of the policies currently in place, over 182 million elementary, middle, and high school students across 198 countries completed the "Hour of Code" tutorials between 2013 and 2015 (Computer Science Education Week, 2016). In January of 2015, the Hour of Code reached 100 million "hours served," making the Hour of Code the largest education campaign in history (Computer Science Education Week, 2016). Furthermore, tools, such as the online Scratch programming community, aimed at creative coders ages 8 and older, has collectively shared 18,345,991 coding projects as of December 2016 (https://scratch.mit.edu/).

According to Code.org, which encourages schools nationwide to adopt programming curricula and promote broad participation in computer science, 71 percent of all new jobs in STEM are in computing. However, only 8 percent of STEM graduates are in computer science. This discrepancy highlights the importance of starting early: the workforce needs coders. And this need is only growing: the U.S. Bureau of Labor Statistics predicts that employment of computer and information technology occupations will grow 12 percent from 2014 to 2024 (U.S. Bureau of Labor Statistics, 2016). This increase represents the fastest average for all occupations, projected to add about 488,500 new jobs in the 20-year span.

Despite this need, this book does not advocate for coding in early childhood as a way to fulfill the workforce's demands. This book proposes that coding is a new literacy for the twenty-first century. As a literacy, coding enables new ways of thinking and new ways of communicating and expressing ideas. Furthermore, literacy ensures participation in decision-making processes and civic institutions. From an historical perspective, and currently in the developing world, those who can't read and write are left out of power structures. Their civic voices are not heard. Will this be the case for those who can't code? For those who can't think in computational ways?

We start teaching kids to read and write in early childhood. However, we don't expect every child to grow into a professional writer. I believe textual literacy is both an important skill and intellectual tool for everyone. So it is with coding. I do not advocate for all children to grow into software engineers and programmers, but I want them to have computational literacy so they can become producers, and not only consumers, of digital artifacts.

While to date most nationwide coding initiatives target older children, there are new endeavors focusing on early childhood education. For example, in April 2016, the White House launched a STEM (science, technology, engineering, and math) initiative for early education (White House, 2016) by convening researchers, policy makers, industry, and educators. As part of this group, I was invited to discuss the role of coding and computational thinking (White House Symposium on Early STEM, see: www.youtube.com/watch?v=iUvEks2tutw&feature=youtu.be&t=36m). Countries such as the United Kingdom have adapted their curriculum to include coding, beginning in early childhood. In Asia, Singapore is currently launching nationwide projects to bring programming through a PlayMaker initiative that brings KIBO robotics, amongst other technologies, into early childhood classrooms (Digital News Asia, 2015; Sullivan & Bers, 2017). Chapter 10 will describe this initiative.

Only recently has there been emphasis on integrating computing in the early years due to the development of new programming interfaces, such as ScratchJr and KIBO, and a growing body of research that suggests children who are exposed to STEM curriculum and computer programming at an early age demonstrate fewer gender-based stereotypes regarding STEM careers (Metz, 2007; Steele, 1997) and fewer obstacles entering technical fields (Madill et al., 2007; Markert, 1996).

Research shows that both from an economic and a developmental standpoint, educational interventions that begin in early childhood are associated with lower costs and more durable effects than interventions that start later on (e.g., Cunha & Heckman, 2007; Heckman & Masterov, 2004). Two National Research Council reports—*Eager to Learn* (2001) and *From Neurons to Neighborhoods* (2002)—document the significance of early experiences for later school achievement. For example, literacy research shows that the foundation for reading success is formed long before a child reaches first grade and that children who fail and do not improve by the end of first grade are at high risk of failure in other academics throughout school (Learning First Alliance, 1998; McIntosh, Horner, Chard, Boland, & Good, 2006). Will the same be true for coding?

I understand the cognitive and economic benefits that underlie the push for introducing coding in early childhood education, and I am happy to see computer programing becoming popular again. However, in this book I build a different case for coding. Not only is it important for children to start programming at a young age to prepare them for the booming computing workforce, but most importantly, coding provides a systematic way of thinking and a language for expression and communication. While coding, children learn to become better problem solvers, mathematicians, engineers, story tellers, inventors, and collaborators. These individual and interpersonal skills are introduced and refined through the process of sequencing a simple program: a kitten appearing and disappearing on a screen, or robots dancing the Hokey Pokey alongside a kindergarten class.

Coding engages and reinforces computational thinking. At the same time, computational thinking engages and reinforces coding. In this context, coding is the action of putting together sequences of instructions and debugging or problem solving when things do not work as expected. In the process (note that coding is a verb, not a noun, so it implies unfolding over time), children encounter powerful ideas from computer science and thus engage in computational thinking. Is coding the only way to engage in this kind of thinking? Definitely not. As we will see later in this book, there are approaches to do so through low-tech games, singing, and dancing. However, in this book, I advocate that coding should be part of every young child's computational thinking experience. Furthermore, I also advocate for a playground approach to coding, as opposed to a playpen experience.

After this introduction, the book has three parts: Part I: Coding as Playground; Part II: Computational Thinking; and Part III: New languages for young children. Throughout the book I present vignettes of children and teachers, as well as results from different studies, theoretical frameworks, technology designs, and curriculum recommendations. I will challenge the reader to think about the many ways that coding can engage young children in some of the same developmental milestones as the playground experience. New initiatives for introducing coding and computational thinking in early childhood education are growing. New standards and frameworks are being developed alongside new programming languages and interfaces. It is our responsibility to make sure that the emphasis on play and creativity, social and emotional growth, are not left out when computer programming enters kindergarten.

References

A Framework for K12 Computer Science Education. (2016). *A Framework for K12 computer science education.* N.p. Web. 13 July 2016. Retrieved from https://k12cs.org/about/

Australian Curriculum Assessment and Reporting Authority. (2015). *Digital technologies: Sequence.* Retrieved from www.acara.edu.au/_resources/ Digital_Technologies_-_Sequence_of_content.pdf

Balanskat, A., & Engelhardt, K. (2015). *Computing our future.* Computer programming and coding. Priorities, school curricula and initiatives across Europe. European Schoolnet, Brussels.

Barron, B., Cayton-Hodges, G., Bofferding, L., Copple, C., Darling-Hammond, L., & Levine, M. (2011). *Take a giant step: A blueprint for teaching children in a digital age.* New York: The Joan Ganz Cooney Center at Sesame Workshop.

Bers, M. U. (2008). *Blocks, robots and computers: Learning about technology in early childhood.* New York: Teacher's College Press.

Bers, M. U. (2012). *Designing digital experiences for positive youth development: From playpen to playground.* Cary, NC: Oxford.

Bers, M. U., Seddighin, S., & Sullivan, A. (2013). Ready for robotics: Bringing together the T and E of STEM in early childhood teacher education. *Journal of Technology and Teacher Education, 21*(3), 355–377.

Code.org. (2016). *Promote computer science.* Retrieved from https://code.org/promote

Computer Science Education Week. (2016). Retrieved from https://csedweek.org/

Cunha, F., & Heckman, J. (2007). The technology of skill formation. *American Economic Review, 97*(2), 31–47.

DevTech Research Group. (2016). Retrieved from ase.tufts.edu/devtech/

Digital News Asia. (2015). *IDA launches S$1.5m pilot to roll out tech toys for preschoolers.*

Elkin, M., Sullivan, A., & Bers, M. U. (2014). Implementing a robotics curriculum in an early childhood Montessori classroom. *Journal of Information Technology Education: Innovations in Practice, 13*, 153–169.

European Schoolnet. (2014). *Computing our future: Computer programming and coding.* Belgium: European Commission.

Heckman, J. J., & Masterov, D. V. (2004). The productivity argument for investing in young children. Technical Report Working Paper No. 5, Committee on Economic Development.

ISTE (International Society for Technology in Education). (2007). *NETS for students 2007 profiles.* Washington, DC: ISTE. Retrieved from www.iste.org/standards/netsforstudents/netsforstudents2007profiles.aspx#PK2

Kazakoff, E. R., & Bers, M. U. (2014). Put your robot in, Put your robot out: Sequencing through programming robots in early childhood. *Journal of Educational Computing Research, 50*(4).

Learning First Alliance. (1998). Every child reading: An action plan of the Learning First Alliance. *American Educator, 22*(1–2), 52–63.

Lifelong Kindergarten Group. (2016). *Scratch.* Retrieved from https://llk.media.mit.edu/projects/783/

Livingstone, I. (2012). Teach children how to write computer programs. *The Guardian.* Guardian News and Media. Retrieved from www.theguardian.com/commentisfree/2012/jan/11/teachchildrencomputer programmes

Madill, H., Campbell, R. G., Cullen, D. M., Armour, M. A., Einsiedel, A. A., Ciccocioppo, A. L., & Coffin, W. L. (2007). Developing career commitment in STEM-related fields: Myth versus reality. In R. J. Burke, M. C. Mattis, & E. Elgar (Eds.), *Women and minorities in science, technology, engineering and mathematics: Upping the numbers* (pp. 210–244). Northhampton, MA: Edward Elgar Publishing.

Markert, L. R. (1996). Gender related to success in science and technology. *The Journal of Technology Studies, 22*(2), 21–29.

McIntosh, K., Horner, R. H., Chard, D. J., Boland, J. B., & Good III, R. H. (2006). The use of reading and behavior screening measures to predict nonresponse to schoolwide positive behavior support: A longitudinal analysis. *School Psychology Review, 35*(2), 275.

Metz, S. S. (2007). Attracting the engineering of 2020 today. In R. Burke & M. Mattis (Eds.), *Women and minorities in science, technology, engineering and mathematics: Upping the numbers* (pp. 184–209). Northampton, MA: Edward Elgar Publishing.

National Association for the Education of Young Children (NAEYC) & Fred Rogers Center. (2012). *Technology and interactive media as tools in early childhood programs serving children from birth through age 8.* Retrieved from www.naeyc.org/files/naeyc/file/positions/PS_technology_WEB2.pdf

Sesame Workshop. (2009). *Sesame workshop and the PNC Foundation join White House effort on STEM education.* Retrieved from www.sesame workshop.org/newsandevents/pressreleases/stemeducation_11212009

Siu, K., & Lam, M. (2003). Technology education in Hong Kong: International implications for implementing the "Eight Cs" in the early childhood curriculum. *Early Childhood Education Journal, 31*(2), 143–150.

Smith, M. (2016). Computer science for all. *The White House blog.* Retrieved from www.whitehouse.gov/blog/2016/01/30/computerscienceall

Steele, C. M. (1997). A threat in the air: How stereotypes shape intellectual identity and performance. *American Psychologist, 52*, 613–629.

Sullivan, A., & Bers, M. U. (2015). Robotics in the early childhood classroom: Learning outcomes from an 8-week robotics curriculum in pre-kindergarten through second grade. *International Journal of Technology and Design Education.* Online First.

Sullivan, A., & Bers, M. U. (2017). Dancing robots Integrating art, music, and robotics in Singapore's early childhood centers. *International Journal of Technology & Design Education.* Online First. doi:10.1007/s10798-017-9397-0

U.S. Bureau of Labor Statistics. (2016). *Computer and information technology occupations.* Retrieved from www.bls.gov/ooh/computerandinfor mationtechnology/home.htm

U.S. Department of Education, Office of Educational Technology. (2010). *Transforming American education: Learning powered by technology.* Washington, DC. Retrieved from www.ed.gov/technology/netp2010

White House. (2016). *Fact sheet: Advancing active STEM education for our youngest learners.* Retrieved from www.whitehouse.gov/thepress office/2016/04/21/factsheetadvancingactivestemeducationouryoungest learners

PART

I

Coding as Playground

In the Beginning There Was Language

In 1969, a young woman named Cynthia Solomon and MIT professor Seymour Papert went to the Muzzey Jr. High School in Lexington, MA, a Boston suburb, to teach students how to program. At the time, "programming" was a strange word and very few people knew what it meant. Although the students were learning programming, there was no computer to be found in the classroom. The computer was a few miles away at the Bolt, Beranek and Newman (BBN) research lab, and the classroom had teletypes, which resembled big typing machines. The information was sent over to a big computer, a PDP1, one of the first modern commercial computers, back at BBN. This was a dedicated LOGO timeshared system. Users saved and retrieved their work sitting at teletype terminals. Although expensive and huge, the PDP1 had computing power equivalent to a 1996 pocket organizer and a little less memory, and it used punched paper tape as its primary storage medium. In its basic form, the PDP1 sold for $120,000 (roughly equivalent to $950,000 today) (Hafner & Lyon, 1996).

Despite all of this, children were invited to use it, to become programmers. Solomon describes how the children "made up hilarious sentence generators and became proficient users of their own math quizzes." This was the beginning of the first programming language for children, LOGO. Led by Seymour Papert at MIT and Wally Feurzeig and Dan Bobrow at BBN, over time, many people contributed and developed different versions of this child friendly version of the LISP programming language. The home for this work was the MIT Artificial Intelligence (AI) Lab, then codirected by Seymour Papert and Marvin Minsky. Thus, it is not surprising that LISP is by some the favored programming language for AI. By 1969, the LOGO group at MIT had been formed, with Papert as its director. As new versions of LOGO were developed, researchers would go to schools to teach and observe what happened in the classroom. Inspired by the Piagetian tradition, they documented their observations in several dozen LOGO memos later published by MIT (MIT LOGO memos, 1971–1981).

"By the 1970–71 school year we had a floor turtle and a display turtle," recalls Solomon in her wiki (Solomon, 2010). While the floor turtle had to be attached to a terminal and children shared it, the display turtle was designed to let users at four different terminals alternately take control of the turtle. By then, LOGO, the first programming language specifically designed for children, included a way to write stories, a way to draw with a programmable object (i.e., the turtle), a way to have the programmable object explore the environment, and a way to make and play music. As early as 1970, the first programming language for children provided tools for creative expression, and not only for problem solving.

Because Seymour Papert was trained as a mathematician, he could see the potential for LOGO to help children understand mathematical ideas by playing with them. He also realized the value of the two different interfaces: the screen-based turtle and the floor-based turtle. The floor turtle would, decades later, evolve into the LEGO® MINDSTORMS® robotics concept through a partnership between the LEGO company and MIT. The onscreen turtle became available through different venues, both commercially and free (i.e., Terrapin Logo, Turtle Logo, Kinderlogo). Geometry and LOGO were a natural match. The children could program the turtle to do anything they wanted. Instructions were given to the turtle to move about in space, and the turtle dragged a pen to draw a trail. Such drawings gave birth to turtle geometry (see Figure 1.1). The turtle could draw squares, rectangles, and circles of all sizes, inviting children to explore the concept of angles. Through coding, mathematics became playful and expressive. Back in those early days, Seymour and his colleagues already wanted children to learn how to code so they could become creators.

"Forward 60, right 90." How many times does this procedure need to be repeated to draw a square? And how should it be adapted to draw a rectangle? While exploring these questions, children would solve multiple problems. However, LOGO engaged children in creating beautiful shapes, not calculating angles. They needed math to make a project of their choice. They learned to see math as a useful, creative tool.

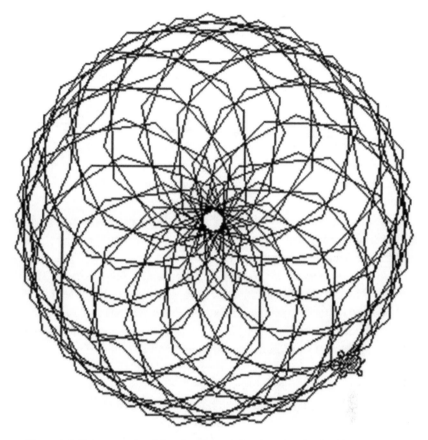

Figure 1.1 This example of "turtle geometry" was created using Terrapin Logo using the following code: Repeat 44 [fd 77 lt 17 repeat 17 [fd 66 rt 49]].

The story of LOGO is also the story of how, for those early researchers devoted to bringing the power of computation to education, programming was associated with children's ability to make something they cared about. They provided tools that offered multiple paths for expression: drawing, storytelling, games, and music. Programming was at the service of expression. Back then, researchers would have flinched at the idea of only associating coding with STEM (science, technology, engineering, and math). Those disciplines provide important skill sets and knowledge, but programming takes the young coder beyond: it provides a tool for personal, communicative expression.

Constructionism

Back in the late '90s, when I was a doctoral student working with Seymour Papert at the MIT Media Lab, the joke was that Seymour did not come in the LOGO box. What we meant was that although we were bringing LOGO and its full expressive potential to schools, many teachers tended to use LOGO in traditional instructionist ways. Creativity and personal expression were left out. Our internal joke hid our wish to have Seymour come inside the LOGO box, so when we needed to convince teachers to let their students freely explore and create a project of their choice, he would come out and help us with his charming personality.

We spent hours sharing his theory, philosophy, and pedagogical approach with as many teachers as we could find. Seymour did not come in the LOGO box, but Constructionism, the framework he developed, came in a book, "*Mindstorms: Children, Computers and Powerful Ideas*" (Papert, 1980). This wonderful book summarizes Papert's approach to how children can become better learners and thinkers through coding. LOGO was carefully designed so young children could create their own personally meaningful projects. However, a top-down curriculum and an instructionist pedagogy could turn LOGO into a completely different tool in classrooms where teachers did not understand the principles of Constructionism. Although LOGO was designed as a playground it could easily become a playpen. Seymour's choice of this word, Constructionism, to name his pedagogical and philosophical approach is a play on Piaget's Constructivism (Ackermann, 2001; Papert & Harel, 1991). Seymour had worked with Jean Piaget in Switzerland and, amongst many things, he understood the importance of learning by doing.

While Piaget's theory explains how knowledge is constructed in our heads through a process of accommodation and assimilation, Papert pays particular attention to the role of computationally rich constructions in the world, as a support for those in the head. Papert's Constructionism asserts that computers are powerful educational technologies when used as tools for creating projects people truly care about. Programming is a vehicle for creation, either on a screen or in the physical world, as shown by the early work on LOGO with both turtle interfaces. Papert's Constructionism believes that independent learning and discovery happen best when children can make, create, program, and design their own "objects to think with" in a playful manner (Bers, 2008). Computational objects can help us think about powerful computational ideas, such as sequencing, abstraction, and modularity, but they also provide an opportunity to communicate our own voices. Coding, then, becomes both a vehicle for new forms of thinking and expression of the resulting thoughts. Chapters 5 and 6 will look at this and explore the powerful ideas of computer science that coding reveals.

Constructionism is my intellectual home. It is from there that I write this book. I apply what is useful to early childhood education and I extend it with my own theoretical framework, which I call Positive Technological Development (PTD). Chapter 8 will expand on this.

Seymour Papert refused to give a definition of Constructionism. In 1991, he wrote, "*It would be particularly oxymoronic to convey the idea of constructionism through a definition since, after all, constructionism boils down to demanding that everything be understood by being constructed*" (Papert, 1991). Respecting his wish, in my past writings I have always avoided providing a definition; however, I have presented four basic principles of Constructionism that have served early childhood education well (Bers, 2008):

1. Learning by designing personally meaningful projects to share in the community;

2. Using concrete objects to build and explore the world;

3. Identifying powerful ideas from the domain of study;

4. Engaging in self-reflection as part of the learning process.

These principles are consistent with the general agreement in early childhood education about the efficacy of "learning by doing" and engaging in "project-based learning" (Diffily & Sassman, 2002; Krajcik & Blumenfeld, 2006). Constructionism extends these approaches to also engage children in "learning by designing" and "learning by programming." From a Constructionist perspective, there is a continuum of learning opportunities that spans from blocks to robots (Bers, 2008). For example, while wooden blocks can help children explore size and shape, robots allow exploration of digital concepts, such as sensors. Nowadays, these are found in most "smart objects" around us, from water dispensers to elevator doors. The early childhood curriculum is supposed to focus on children's experiences in the world, and smart objects like these are a growing presence in our world.

When children are provided tools to learn about these "smart objects" by making them, fixing them, or playing with them through educational robotics, they not only become producers of their own projects, but they also explore disciplinary realms of knowledge, such as coding and engineering, as well as the nature of knowledge itself. They "think about thinking." They become epistemologists, just like Piaget who was deeply interested in the nature of knowledge, and just like Papert, who named his research group at the MIT Media Lab "Epistemology and Learning."

In Memoriam

Seymour Papert was a South African mathematician who worked with Jean Piaget in Geneva and then moved to Boston and became the co-director of the Artificial Intelligence (AI) Lab at MIT. He was one of the founding pioneers of the MIT Media Lab. After he died in July 2016, Gary Stager wrote a beautiful obituary for *Nature*: "Few academics of Papert's stature have spent as much time as he did working in real schools. He delighted in the theories, ingenuity and playfulness of children. Tinkering or programming with them was the cause of many missed meetings" (Stager, 2016). I recall those missed meetings with frustration. I was an eager student trying to make sense of many questions.

Seymour loved questions but he did not have enough hours in the day to explore them all. By the time I met him, Seymour was already a prominent figure and embarked on frequent trips. So, escorting him to the airport was a wonderful and rare opportunity to have his undivided attention. He was always travelling, so such meetings became frequent. I remember discussing my questions in the back of a taxi or an airport coffee shop while he was waiting for his next plane. I also remember having to interrupt a thought provoking discussion because his flight was leaving.

Seymour was a man of ideas. I believe he fell in love with computer programming because of its potential to bring about new ideas, both at the personal and societal level. Ideas can change the world, and Seymour wanted to change the world. In that sense, Seymour and the Constructionist tradition have much in common with literacy. The advent of mass literacy was a world changing event. Literacy is not only an "instrumental" tool, but also an "epistemological tool" that restructures the way we know the world. Will computational literacy become the new literacy of the twenty-first century? The next chapter will explore the concept of coding as a literacy.

References

Ackermann, E. (2001). Piaget's Constructivism, Papert's Constructionism: What's the difference? *Future of Learning Group Publication, 5*(3), 438.

Bers, M. U. (2008). *Blocks to robots: Learning with technology in the early childhood classroom.* New York, NY: Teachers College Press.

Diffily, D., & Sassman, C. (2002). *Project based learning with young children.* 88 Post Road West, PO Box 5007, Westport, CT 06881–5007: Heinemann, Greenwood Publishing Group, Inc.

Hafner, K., & Lyon, M. (1996). *Where wizards stay up late: The origins of the Internet* (1st Touchstone ed.). New York: Simon and Schuster.

Krajcik, J. S., & Blumenfeld, P. (2006). Project based learning. In R. K. Sawyer (Ed.), *Cambridge handbook of the learning sciences* (pp. 317–333). New York: Cambridge University Press.

MIT LOGO Memos. (1971–1981). *Memo collection.* Retrieved from www.sonoma.edu/users/l/luvisi/logo/logo.memos.html

Papert, S., & Harel, I. (1991). Situating constructionism. *Constructionism, 36*(2), 1–11.

Rinaldi, C. (1998). Projected curriculum constructed through documentation— Progettazione: An interview with Lella Gandini. In C. Edwards, L. Gandini, & G. Forman (Eds.), *The hundred languages of children: The Reggio Emilia approach—Advanced reflections* (2nd ed., pp. 113–125). Greenwich, CT: Ablex.

Solomon, C. (2010). *Logo, Papert and Constructionist learning.* Retrieved November 15, 2016, from http://logothings.wikispaces.com/

Stager, G. S. (2016). Seymour Papert (1928–2016). *Nature, 537*(7620), 308.

2 Coding as Literacy

Coding is the new literacy. Since the early '60s, computer advocates have claimed that reading and writing code resembles textual literacy in many ways. Both computational and textual literacy empower individuals to think and express themselves. In this chapter I will unpack the concept of coding as literacy by looking at the societal and historical aspects as well as the cognitive theories aimed at understanding literacy.

Scholars in literacy studies have defined literacy as a human faculty with a symbolic and infrastructural technology—such as a textual writing system—that can be used for creative, communicative, and rhetorical purposes. Literacy enables people to represent their ideas in texts that can travel away from immediate, interpersonal contexts (to write) and to interpret texts produced by others (to read) (Vee, 2013). To achieve literacy, we need technologies. The Merriam-Webster Dictionary defines technology as "the practical application of knowledge especially in a particular area." Reading and writing are technologies of textual literacy, while coding is a technology of computational literacy. Each of these technologies is associated with particular tools, and tools can be defined as implements that support or enable the use of the symbolic or infrastructural technologies. For example, the tool of the printing press served to spread textual literacy to the masses, and programming languages support the development of computational literacy. Orality, the historical period before literacy, also had its own tools: voice and gestures.

Walter Ong was an American Jesuit priest and scholar who explored how the transition from orality to literacy influenced culture, but also how it changed human consciousness. In his seminal work *Orality and Literacy: The Technologizing of the Word* (Ong, 1982), Ong studies societies that are transitioning from orality to literacy (especially writing and print) and suggests a fundamental shift in the form of thought. "Without writing, the literate mind would not and could not think as it does, not only when engaged in writing but even when it is composing its thoughts in oral form . . . The fact that we do not commonly feel the influence of writing on our thoughts shows that we have interiorized the technology of writing so deeply that without tremendous effort we cannot separate it from ourselves or even recognize its presence and influence" (Ong, 1986, p. 24).

Ong describes writing as a technology that must be learned and that initiates the transformation of thinking from the world of sound to the world of sight. For example, oral cultures might not understand the concept of "looking up something." It would have no meaning because, without writing, words have no visual presence, even when the objects they represent are visual. Words are sounds, and visual metaphors can't describe them. Spoken words happen in time, not in space.

Oral cultures require mnemotechnic strategies for preserving information over time in the absence of writing. For example, they rely on proverbs, condensed wisdom, epic poetry, and characters. These oral cultures favor cyclic thought. The shaman or storyteller invites people to hear stories, which are told in cyclical, redundant ways to aid with memory. Instead, cultures of literacy favor linear, logical, historical, or evolutionary thought, which depend on writing. Ong was particularly interested in cultures in a transition phase from orality to literacy and he pointed out how early criticism of computers has similarities to early criticism of writing (Ong, 1982).

This line of work looks at literacy as an historical and social phenomenon with strong epistemological implications. The technologies of writing, which have changed over time, have impacted the way we think about the world. For example, the printing press facilitated the wide distribution of ideas, while the early scribe kept knowledge isolated and for just a few chosen readers. Furthermore, writing restructures our thinking. Fundamentally, the technologies of writing support logical sequential thinking and allow the separation of the subject from the object (i.e., of what is told from who is telling it). The object (the written text) takes a life of its own and can be analyzed, deconstructed, and interpreted. This brings about metacognition: "thinking about thinking." Seymour Papert used to say that "you can't think about thinking without thinking about thinking about something" (Papert, 2005). He was referring to the importance of the metacognitive level, of understanding our own way of knowing and making sense of the world. In his view, the computer, and the ability to program it, provided

25

an opportunity for children to create "something" (i.e., a computational project) for thinking about thinking. Both the written text and the computational project provide an opportunity for metacognition, for deconstructing and interpreting our own thinking in the process of making them.

For example, a child who uses LOGO to make a game to teach young children about fractions is not only thinking about computer science and mathematics, but is also thinking about game design principles and perspective. The child needs to think about the kind of background knowledge the users will have and adapt the game accordingly; they need to think about color preferences and make interface design choices to keep users engaged. This child programmer puts herself in the shoes of the gamer and tries to understand how he or she would likely react when encountering a new challenge. We know, from long-standing research on cognitive development, that perspective taking is fundamental for thinking (Tjosvold & Johnson, 1978; Tudge & Rogoff, 1999; Tudge & Winterhoff, 1993; Walker, 1980). This child programmer was not asked to "think about thinking" in a vacuum. That task is very difficult, if not impossible. They had created something to think about: an interactive fractions game. Throughout the process of using LOGO to program the fraction game to teach others, the child developed "computational literacy" (DiSessa, 2001). However, perhaps most importantly, the child can become an epistemologist and further explore how knowledge is constructed, and how we learn what we learn (Turkle, 1984).

Textual and Computational Literacy

The computational project created by a child, as well as the text written by an author, both products of literacy, are independent from the creator and take on lives of their own. These artifacts can be shared, read, revised, and played with. They evoke an emotional response. Once out in the world, the artifact can be interpreted differently than the original intent of the author. The child who coded the game and the author of a text have no control over how their products will be received by others. The process of creation is iterative: problems are encountered and solved along the way. The child coder finds bugs in the program and fixes them. The author finds grammatical errors and leaps of thought. Revising and editing become major tasks in textual literacy, much like debugging in computational literacy.

In this process—starting with an original idea and ending with a sharable product (i.e., a computer game or a text)—the creative and the critical processes need each other. Papert quotes T. S. Eliot to make this point: "*The large part of the labor of an author in composing his work is critical labor; the labor of sifting, combining, constructing, expunging, correcting, testing; this frightful toil is as much critical as creative.*" The artifact detached from its creator becomes powerful in its own right. However, it can sometimes hide the process of its creation. As we will see in future chapters, when working with computational literacy, we must move the process of programming to the forefront. Coding is the journey that takes us to making a final artifact. We are as interested in the journey as in the outcome.

In early childhood education, there is a strong tradition around documenting process. For example, the Reggio Emilia approach to education focuses on intensively documenting children's experiences, memories, thoughts, and ideas during their work, not just the completed outcome (Katz & Chard, 1996). Documentation may include samples of a child's work at several different stages of completion, photographs showing work in progress, feedback written by the teacher, and even comments made by parents or other children. Documentation makes the hidden learning process transparent. It invites the revisiting of a created artifact to understand the path to its creation.

Similarly, the field of literacy studies aims to bring the hidden process of writing to the surface. Different sources are employed to reconstruct the journey that led the author to write the book, and to unpack its structure and mechanics. The nascent field of computational literacy aims to understand the journey of encountering computational thinking in the process of coding or creating a sharable project.

Back in 1987, Papert called for the development of a field of study, which he called "computer criticism," by analogy with literary criticism. He wrote: "The name does not imply that such writing would condemn computers any more than literary criticism condemns literature . . . The purpose of computer criticism is not to condemn but to understand, to explicate, to place in perspective" (Papert, 1987, p. 2). Papert envisioned that this new discipline would help better illuminate the present role of computers and computer programming in society, and most specifically, in education.

While computer criticism is in its infancy compared with its sister discipline, the use of literacy as a model for understanding the role of coding is promising. Literacy, like coding, assumes the ability to produce an arti-fact detached from its creator. There is a producer with an intention, with a passion, with a desire to communicate something. Writing, like coding, is a medium for human expression. This perspective is mostly absent in cur-rent conversations that mainly describe coding and computational think-ing as problem-solving processes. Expression requires problem solving as well as a knowledge base; however, problem solving is not the end goal. For example, to make an animation, I need programming skills. I solve problems I encounter along the way, not because I love problem solving (although I might), but because I want to express myself through an exter-nal artifact (an animation) that can be shared and interpreted by others.

Coding as an Expressive Medium

What happens in the head of a child who is coding? What happens in the head of a child who is reading and writing? How are the processes of learn-ing these skills similar or different? To develop written language, we first needed spoken language. Orality came before literacy. What can the field of computational literacy learn from the rich history of textual literacy to support educational interventions?

Jerome Bruner was an American psychologist and scholar who made significant contributions to cognitive psychology and educational theory. When looking at language development, Bruner offered a social interac-tionist perspective (Bruner,1975, 1985). In his approach, the social and interpersonal nature of language was emphasized, in sharp contrast with Noam Chomsky's nativist account of language acquisition (Chomsky, 1976). Inspired by Lev Vygotsky, the Russian theoretician of sociocultural development, Bruner proposed that social interaction plays a fundamental role in the development of cognition in general, and of language in par-ticular. Children learn language to communicate, and, in the process, they learn the linguistic code, including its syntax and grammar. Children are "learning about" and "using" language at the same time. It is difficult to identify which comes first. Of course, children don't do it alone; they have the aid (or scaffold) of peers, adults, games, and songs. In the same spirit, in the "coding as a playground" approach I propose, children learn to code and use the code in their own projects at the same time. Fluency develops with use.

To Bruner, the desired outcomes of learning were not just the language concepts and categories, neither the mastery of problem solving procedures invented previously by the culture through grammatical and syntactic rules, but the ability of children to invent these things for themselves and apply what they have learned to different contexts. For example, using written language to write an invitation or a book, or using coding to make an animation or a geometrical shape. The goal of teaching coding is not syntactic mastery of a programming language, but the ability to create one's own meaningful and unique project. The act of coding may facilitate computational thinking, but it doesn't always: we are all familiar with examples in which children are asked to copy code from the blackboard and memorize syntactic rules without engaging in thinking. As a literacy, coding involves doing, creating, and making, not just thinking. It involves the production of an external sharable artifact.

In early childhood, coding assumes the understanding that there is a language that represents actions (computational instructions) and that the language can be used to create projects by combining the computational instructions in new ways. As children grow and learn more sophisticated programming languages, coding also involves playing with grammatical rules and discovering new syntax. Often, when coding "goes to school," it is in the form of challenges or logical puzzles to solve. Teachers assign the problems and students need to solve them. Such are most experiences of students who have been exposed to traditional computer science classes. While this might work well for children who are intrinsically motivated, unfortunately, the lack of opportunities for self-expression turns off many. My approach is different: the goal of coding is expression, not problem solving. Problem solving is a tool for expression. We have something to say, a project to show, an idea to explore, and we do it through making a personally meaningful project to share with others.

Programming languages that are developmentally appropriate for young children must support children's expression. Isn't the developmental task of the young child to start finding his or her own voice in the world? For example, a child can use ScratchJr to create an animated birthday card for her dad or program KIBO to dance to the beat of her favorite song. In the process, the child is learning powerful concepts and skills from computer science, and doing a lot of problem solving. Although problem solving is not the only goal of coding in early childhood, it is a powerful mechanism that allows children to express themselves and communicate.

Mitchel Resnick and David Siegel, when discussing the creation of the Scratch Foundation in 2013 to promote a very different approach to coding, wrote (Resnick & Siegel, 2015):

> For us, coding is not a set of technical skills but a new type of literacy and personal expression, valuable for everyone, much like learning to write. We see coding as a new way for people to organize, express, and share their ideas. . . In many introductory coding activities, students are asked to program the movements of a virtual character navigating through a set of obstacles toward a goal. This approach can help students learn some basic coding concepts, but it doesn't allow them to express themselves creatively—or develop a longterm engagement with coding. It's like offering a writing class that teaches only grammar and punctuation without providing students a chance to write their own stories.
>
> (Resnick & Siegel, 2015, pp. 1–3)

Again, coding is connected to literacy and can be a way to express ourselves. Back in 1987, Seymour Papert promoted the idea of the computer as a medium for human expression. "If it has not yet had its Shakespeares, its Michelangelos or its Einsteins, it will," he promised. Now, almost 20 years later, we can easily identify these Shakespeares, Michelangelos, and Einsteins. They are the creators of innovative programing languages and programmers who became successful entrepreneurs, philanthropists, and business people because they truly understood the societal power of computation.

The Power of Literacy

Computational literacy has historical, social, communicative, and civic commonalities with textual literacy (Vee, 2013). As more people learn to code and computer programming departs the exclusive domain of computer science and becomes central to other professions, the civic dimension of literacy comes into play. We are leaving the scribal age, when literacy was just for a few chosen ones, and entering the printing press era, when it was for the masses. Literacy has the power to bring about social change.

For example, the use of literacy campaigns that mobilize people and resources on a large scale is a long-established practice. H. S. Bhola traces literacy campaigns back to the Protestant Reformation in Europe in the early 1500s (Bhola, 1997). Often, these literacy campaigns supported social, economic, cultural, and political reform or transformation. In the 1970s, mass adult literacy campaigns were commonly initiated by governments following liberation wars with a revolutionary or decolonization agenda (Bhola, 1984).

For example, in the 1960s the Brazilian educator Paulo Freire was commissioned to head the countries' literacy campaign. Freire, most well known for his work on the pedagogy of the oppressed, believed education to be a political act that could not be divorced from pedagogy. Resnick and Siegel talk about how Freire recognized that writing is more than just a practical skill and he led literacy campaigns in poor communities not simply to help people get jobs, but to help people learn that they can make and remake themselves. Freire championed the fact that education should allow the socially, economically, or politically oppressed individuals to regain their sense of humanity, and literacy was his tool. He firmly believed that oppressed individuals must play a role in their own liberation. The first step was teaching reading and writing to all; literacy became a tool of liberation. Literacy provided power intellectually and politically.

In transitioning oral societies, as Walter Ong described, the power resided in those unique individuals or social groups who could read and write and who, later, had the monopoly over printed books. Those who are illiterate are disenfranchised. The phrase "coding as literacy" means not only teaching computer programming with the goal of preparing students for computer science degrees and careers (due to the shortage of programmers and software developers in the industry), it means giving them the intellectual tools to have a voice and to play a role in civic society. In today's world, those who can produce digital technologies will do better than those who can only consume them. Those who can innovate and problem solve will create the democracies of tomorrow, ready to take on the challenges of a multicultural, multiethnic, multireligious, complex global world.

Coding is more than a technical skill; it is a way to achieve literacy in the twenty-first century, like reading and writing. It can change not only the way we think about our own thinking, but also the way we see ourselves in society and the way we construct the legal and democratic mechanisms for running such a society. It can be used to bring about positive changes. As we will see in future chapters, the PTD (Positive Technological Development) approach that I developed emphasizes the aim of teaching coding so children can become contributors to society. Children can use the technology of coding to make a better and more just world. As educators, we must be aware of this when thinking about pedagogical approaches for teaching coding. If our teaching is limited to puzzle-like challenges, we deprive children of the most powerful impact of computational literacy: expression with their own voices.

The Technologies of Literacy

Inspired by Michel Foucault's philosophical construct of "technologies of the self," I propose that the technologies of literacy, both textual and computational, permit us to: 1) produce and transform artifacts; 2) use sign systems associated with meanings; 3) determine conduct of individuals; and 4) transform our own selves through thoughts (Foucault, Martin, Gutman, & Hutton, 1988). These four elements inform my construct of "coding as literacy." Literacy needs technologies. These technologies allow actions and thinking. Within this definition, technologies allow the transformation of thinking into actions: reading, writing, coding. The technologies of reading and writing vary, and different tools can be used; for example, the printing press supports the mass communication of ideas, while handwritten scrolls assign exclusivity. The pen enables creative expression, but is not great for editing of our writing. The crayon is useful when learning how to make our first letter traces, but not for crafting long essays. The tools for coding also vary and there are myriad programming languages supported by different technical platforms.

How do we choose the best tools to support both textual and computational literacy? How do we design new ones that are developmentally appropriate? Early childhood researchers have spent decades understanding the best tools for supporting children's writing (Dyson, 1982; Graham, McKeown, Kiuhara, & Harris, 2012; Graham & Perin, 2007; Graves, 1994; Taylor, 1983). Educators carefully choose the best writing tools for their young students and make recommendations to parents. In the same spirit, the nascent field of early childhood technology must make informed choices regarding developmentally appropriate programming languages and platforms for children.

It is not only the responsibility of professionals in software engineering to design the tools for computational literacy. Those of us with an understanding of learning and child development theories must work together with them. This interdisciplinary endeavor can only be possible if we learn to speak each other's languages and encounter each other's ideas. I devoted two decades of my life to this, hoping to cultivate the new generation of scholars and practitioners who can be at ease in both worlds. For example, my DevTech research group at Tufts includes students from varied disciplines such as cognitive science, education, child development, mechanical engineering, human factors, computer science, and education, just to name a few.

In the last part of the book, I will present two programming languages that my DevTech group has designed and developed over the years with a wonderful team of collaborators: ScratchJr and KIBO robotics. I will also propose design principles for those who are interested in being part of the conversation of what is needed, from a child development and learning perspective, when creating new languages. It is my vision that as the field matures, many different programming languages specifically designed for young children will become available. Each of them will display unique interfaces to support and promote new ways of expression. For now, the next chapter will explore what makes a programming language a unique technology for computational literacy.

References

Bhola, H. S. (1984). *Campaigning for literacy: Eight national experiences of the twentieth century, with a memorandum to decision makers.* Paris: UNESCO.

Bhola, H. S. (1997). What happened to the mass campaigns on their way to the twenty-first century? *NORRAG, Norrag News, 21,* August 1997, 27–29. Retrieved from http://norrag.t3dev1.crossagency.ch/en/publications/norragnews/onlineversion/thefifthinternationalconference onadulteducation/detail/whathappenedtothemasscampaignsontheirway tothetwentyfirstcentury.html (Accessed 07 March 2014).

Bruner, J. S. (1975). The ontogenesis of speech acts. *Journal of Child Language, 2,* 1–19.

Bruner, J. S. (1985). *Child's talk.* Cambridge: Cambridge University Press.

Chomsky, N. (1976). On the biological basis of language capacities. In *The neuropsychology of language* (pp. 1–24). New York: Springer.

DiSessa, A. A. (2001). *Changing minds: Computers, learning, and literacy.* Cambridge, MA: MIT Press.

Dyson, A. H. (1982). Reading, writing, and language: Young children solving the written language puzzle. *Language Arts, 59*(8), 829–839.

Foucault, M., Martin, L. H., Gutman, H., & Hutton, P. H. (1988). *Technologies of the self: A seminar with Michel Foucault.* Amherst, MA: University of Massachusetts Press.

Graham, S., McKeown, D., Kiuhara, S., & Harris, K. R. (2012). A meta-analysis of writing instruction for students in the elementary grades. *Journal of Educational Psychology, 104*(4), 879.

Graham, S., & Perin, D. (2007). Writing next: Effective strategies to improve writing of adolescents in middle and high schools. A report to Carnegie Corporation of New York. Washington, DC: Alliance for Excellent Education.

Graves, D. H. (1994). *A fresh look at writing.* 361 Hanover St., Portsmouth, NH 03801–3912: Heinemann. (ISBN0435088246, $20).

Katz, L. G., & Chard, S. C. (1996). The contribution of documentation to the quality of early childhood education. ERIC Digest. Champaign, IL: ERIC Clearinghouse on Elementary and Early Childhood Education. ED 393 608.

Ong, W. (1982). *Orality and literacy: The technologizing of the word.* London: Methuen.

Ong, W. (1986). Writing is a technology that restructures thought. In G. Baumann (Ed.), *The written word: Literacy in transition* (pp. 23–50). Oxford: Clarendon Press; New York: Oxford University Press.

Papert, S. (1987). Computer criticism vs. technocentric thinking. *Educational Researcher, 16*(1), 22–30.

Papert, S. (2005). You can't think about thinking without thinking about thinking about something. *Contemporary Issues in Technology and Teacher Education, 5*(3–4), 366–367.

Resnick, M., & Siegel, D (2015 Nov 10). A different approach to coding: How kids are making and remaking themselves from Scratch [Web blog post].

Bright: What's new in education. Retrieved June 29, 2017 from https://brightreads.com/a-different-approach-to-coding-d679b06d83a

Taylor, D. (1983). *Family literacy: Young children learning to read and write.* 70 Court St., Portsmouth, NH 03801: Heinemann Educational Books Inc.

Tjosvold, D., & Johnson, D. W. (1978). Controversy within a cooperative or competitive context and cognitive perspective taking. *Contemporary Educational Psychology, 3*(4), 376–386.

Tudge, J., & Rogoff, B. (1999). Peer influences on cognitive development: Piagetian and Vygotskian perspectives. *Lev Vygotsky: Critical Assessments, 3,* 32–56.

Tudge, J. R., & Winterhoff, P. A. (1993). Vygotsky, Piaget, and Bandura: Perspectives on the relations between the social world and cognitive development. *Human Development, 36*(2), 61–81.

Turkle, S. (1984). *The second self: Computers and the human spirit.* New York: Simon and Schuster.

Vee, A. (2013). Understanding computer programming as a literacy. *Literacy in Composition Studies, 1*(2), 42–64.

Walker, L. J. (1980). Cognitive and perspective taking prerequisites for moral development. *Child Development,* 131–139.

3 | Tools and Language

A pen is a tool. I can write with it. I can write in any language I know. I was born and raised in Argentina, so I can write in Spanish. And, of course, I can write in English; I learned it as a second language before moving to the U.S. for graduate school. I can also write in French and Hebrew. I learned those languages as a child, living in both the Ivory Coast and Israel. Writing in Hebrew is very different than writing in English: I write from right to left, and I do not write the vowels, only the consonants. French has letters and accents that cannot be found in Spanish or English, and sentence structures in English are different than in Spanish or French. Over the years, I have developed textual literacy independent of any written language. I can use the writing system to translate spoken language into symbols that others can read, and I understand the concept of symbolic representation. Each language has its own syntax and grammar, but, since I understand fundamental principles of writing, I can apply those when writing in a new language. My ability to write in a fluent way has influenced my way of thinking. I can think in linear and sequential ways.

If I have a pen and I am fluent with a language of my choice, I can produce different textual artifacts. I can write a love letter, a grant proposal, or a shopping list. I will probably choose Spanish for the first task and English for the second and third tasks. Each language has unique qualities that I believe facilitate my purpose to communicate with others or with myself: my husband is also from Argentina and thus Spanish is our shared language; the funding agency I submit grants to is American; and my everyday life happens predominantly in English, so a shopping list is most efficient in that language. The pen allows the use of language to communicate even when I am not present. I can write with it, but I can also scribble and draw. These are all creative endeavors in which I become a producer of new content. But, I can also use the pen in boring and passive ways. As a child, when learning to spell, I was asked to copy the same word 100 times. My teacher claimed that it was a necessary step to build the required skills. If she had read Bruner, she probably would have realized that it is possible to use language and learn about language at the same time, and she might have chosen a more expressive activity to build and reinforce skills. The pen is a tool. The intention of the user of the tool determines how much creativity is displayed. The pen is a vehicle, a medium, a tool for the written language.

A computer is also a tool. I can do boring or creative things with it. I can become a consumer or a producer of content. I can play computer games or I can make my own games. If I know a programming language, I can code. I can code with ScratchJr, LOGO, or JAVA. I used to code with LISP when I was a graduate student, but I have forgotten it because I have not used it in many years. Each of these programming languages also has its own syntax and grammar, and some are better for certain tasks. If I want to make an animation, I will do it with ScratchJr. If I want to program a recommendation system, such as the one Netflix or Amazon has, I will use JAVA. If I want to make a beautiful drawing with geometrical shapes, I will use LOGO. Over the years I have gained a certain degree of computational literacy. I am not an expert programmer; I could not make a living working as a software engineer, but I know enough to call myself fluent in some of these languages. I can use them for expression and communication.

A tool, like the computer, is not a language, but a language can become a tool when we become fluent in it. A pen is not Spanish; a computer is not LOGO. A tool allows me to use the language to do something; tools and languages are nouns, not verbs. They do not convey actions. Writing and coding are verbs: there is a subject that performs an action. There is intentionality and choice. Like natural written languages, programming languages have syntax and grammar, they are a reliable form of information storage and transfer, and they invite the process of decoding, encoding, reading, and writing. Like natural written languages, they are artificial and need to be taught. In this learning process, one develops new ways of thinking.

The process of writing and the process of coding both lead to the creation of a final product that can be shared with others. The parallels between writing and coding are powerful: both involve comprehension and generation; both welcome different levels of fluency, from beginners to experts; both involve the use of tools and the use of language; both can fulfill the need for expression and communication. Literacy, both textual and computational, doesn't only emerge from knowing how to use the tool, although that is a prerequisite, but also from knowing how to use the language. Beyond literacy, there is a need for fluency and of ease of use. Seymour Papert used to talk about fluency as a skill that allows us to navigate different worlds and still apply our knowledge. For example, when one is fluent in computer programming, one can create many different projects and quickly learn new programming languages. This is only achieved over time and after many struggles; it doesn't come easily. But it can be a lot of fun.

Will Coding Become Obsolete?

Both a written natural language and a programming language provide a physical means for representing symbols of a system in a permanent or semi-permanent medium so they may be interpreted. This can happen visually, with either textual or icon-based interfaces, or in a tactile way. We are most familiar with textual interfaces; however, tactile coding systems have been devised both in writing, such as the Braille system, and in programming, such as KIBO's tangible wooden blocks.

Today we think of coding and programming languages as going hand in hand; this was not always the case. The earliest computers relied on engineering, rather than coding, to program them. Vee (2013) describes how:

> Harvard's Mark I, completed in 1944, was programmed by switching circuits or physically plugging wires into vacuum tubes. Each new calculation required rewiring the machine, essentially making the computer a special purpose machine for each new situation. With the development in 1945 of the 'stored program concept,' the computer's program could be stored in memory in the same way that it stored its data. While simple in hindsight, this design was revelatory—it moved the concept of 'programming' from physical engineering to symbolic representation. Programming became the manipulation of *code*, a symbolic text that was part of a

writing system. In this way, computers became technologies of writing as well as engineering.

(Vee, 2013, p. 48)

However, many believe that programming will soon become obsolete because computers will just understand us in natural language (i.e., Maney, 2014). While this might or might not be true, we will still need the logic, sequencing, decomposition, and problem solving required to give instructions to a computer.

We are still far away from having machines display a full array of artificial intelligence, and humans still need to do much of the thinking. Thus, the question is not whether coding will become obsolete or not, but how we can support computational thinking, regardless of the specifics of the coding system or programming language.

Computational thinking begins with asking a question that can be addressed by "decomposing" big tasks into a logical series of smaller steps, just like a recipe. While programming languages promote computational thinking, there are other unplugged ways, like the popular board game Robot Turtles (Shapiro, 2015). Released in 2013, it is designed for young children ages 3–8 and helps them start thinking in computational ways while playing a traditional turn-based board game. How can young players think in computational ways without a programming language or even a computer? In Robot Turtle, using a variety of "obstacle cards" such as ice walls, crates, and stone walls, the players make a maze on the board that their turtles need to navigate to get to their respective jewels. Children place their turtles in the corners of the game board and their jewels somewhere amidst the maze. The kids play instruction cards one at a time on their turn (such as, turn right, turn left, and move forward) to navigate the obstacles. When they get to their jewel, they win. If they make a mistake at any time, they can just tap the bug card (a whimsical cartoon bug that also represents a "bug" or problem in the code) to fix it and make changes (see Figure 3.1). Because every player is trying to get to their own jewel, every player can find their own way to win. There are multiple paths for reaching a goal and for solving a problem successfully.

The powerful ideas that children encounter while playing this game, such as sequencing and debugging, breaking one big problem into smaller steps, and planning and testing a strategy, tap into the core of computational thinking. Chapter 6 will explore them in depth. In my own

Figure 3.1 The Robot Turtles board game in the middle of a four-person game.

work at the DevTech research group at Tufts University, we have also used low-tech strategies to promote computational thinking: singing and dancing, card games, bingo, and Simon Says. Any approach that encourages sequencing and problem solving is a good precursor for computational thinking.

Software and apps have also been created to encourage computational thinking. For example, Lightbot, a highly rated educational video game (https://lightbot.com/), also uses the idea of navigating a maze (Biggs, 2013; Eaton, 2014). Players arrange symbols on the screen to command Lightbot to walk, turn, jump, switch on a light, and so on. The maze and the list of symbols become more complicated as the game progresses.

However, this kind of software, while it promotes computational thinking and runs on a computer, doesn't engage in the full range of experiences that a programming language does. It focuses on problem solving, but not expression. It facilitates exploration of computational concepts in a limited way. It doesn't support creative projects; it is a playpen, not a playground. As a playpen, it serves a purpose (i.e., practicing skills, mastering discrete concepts, isolating skills), but it shouldn't be confused with a playground and its open-ended opportunities.

Programming languages can become playgrounds in which children code. If designed in a developmentally appropriate way, children can code in a playful way. In the process, they develop computational thinking. But they need to learn the grammar and syntax of the programming language to become fluent. Like writing in Spanish, English, or Hebrew, the language of choice doesn't matter if we are fluent in it and can use it for self-expression and communication. Likewise, programming languages, when one has achieved fluency, support personal expression and communication. Technological fluency is developed only after many attempts at problem solving. In my approach, problem solving is not the goal of teaching a programming language or of promoting computational thinking, but is a necessary step so others can see and understand who we are and what we are making.

Programming Languages for Young Children

Young children, with their own developmental needs and abilities, need programming languages specifically designed for them. Part III of this book will expand on this. These must be simple languages that still support multiple combinations, have syntax and a grammar, and offer multiple ways to solve a problem. They must be playgrounds, not playpens. They need to provide opportunities for creating a computational artifact that can be shared with others and support a growing range of computational literacy skills, from beginners to experts. A child who is fluent in a particular programming language is more likely to learn a second one with ease. This child has probably mastered some aspects of computational thinking and can transfer that mastery to different situations.

In the last few years, several programming language and robotic systems specifically designed for young children have come to market. I have personally been involved with two of them: ScratchJr and KIBO. Chapters 9 and 10 describe them both in depth and, throughout the book, several vignettes depict children's experiences with them in a variety of early childhood settings. For now, the following vignettes describe young children's experiences while learning and playing with other existing tools and their encounters with the powerful ideas of computer science and computational thinking.

Exploring Control Structures With Daisy

Sean has been working with Daisy the Dinosaur in his first grade classroom for a couple of weeks when his mother decides to download the app on her iPad. She wants him to practice programming at home. Daisy the Dinosaur is a free app that allows children to explore programming by making a green and pink dinosaur named Daisy move around onscreen (daisythedinosaur.com). Daisy can be programmed through two modes: a structured challenge mode and a free play mode. Like ScratchJr, the app has simple but playful graphics that are appealing for young children. It has limited instructions so children can jump into coding right away. Children explore foundational coding by programming Daisy to complete simple actions such as move, spin, jump, and roll. Advanced coding can be explored using Daisy's "when" and "repeat" commands. One of the key differences between Daisy the Dinosaur and ScratchJr is that ScratchJr's programming blocks are graphical and require no reading. Daisy the Dinosaur, on the other hand, requires reading simple words such as "turn" and "shrink" in each programming block.

At first, Sean's mom sets the app to "Challenge Mode." She wants to know how much he can do. Sean has explored most of these challenges at school and cruises through them quickly to show his mom that he is ready for the "Free Play" mode. This allows him to program Daisy to do whatever he wants. He makes Daisy spin, walk around, grow, and shrink onscreen. Because the app requires some reading, especially when it comes to the programming blocks, his mom sits with him to refresh his memory on the words' meanings. Eventually, his mother leaves him alone.

Around 15 minutes later, to his mother's delight, Sean says he's programmed a magic trick for her to see. "I'm the magician and I can make my dinosaur Daisy turn into a super gigantic dragon!" he explains. "How can you do that?" his mom asks. "With just the touch of my finger and the magic word: Abracadabra!" Sean taps Daisy and she grows very large. "See?" He says proudly, showing off his code. "I just learned this new block called 'When,' and Daisy only grows when I tap her. We didn't learn this one at school." Sean's mom is impressed by his imagination and his ability to naturally master a new concept just by having free time to play and explore on his own.

Sean has encountered control structures. He is learning that he can control when or if something happens to Daisy based on the state of his iPad. This is a very powerful concept in computer science. He shows his mom how he can start a program by touching Daisy or even by shaking the iPad. Sean cannot wait to tell his friends at school all about the new blocks he learned!

Sequencing With a Bee

Suzy is a 5-year-old kindergartener who loves mazes. Each day during choice time she draws mazes out on paper for her friends to solve or explores activity books that have mazes in them. On Tuesday morning, Suzy's teacher, Mrs. McKinnon, reveals a big surprise to the kids at circle time: the class will be getting a new robot friend named BeeBot! BeeBot is a robot that resembles a yellow and black bumblebee (www.beebot.us). BeeBot has directional keys on its back that are used to enter up to 40 commands which send BeeBot forward, back, left, and right. Pressing the green Go button starts BeeBot on its way. Mrs. McKinnon gives the class a demo of BeeBot. She tells them that during choice time, she will bring students one at a time to help program BeeBot to move along the path on a colorful floor map.

Later that day, during choice time, Suzy is happily scribbling away at a maze when Mrs. McKinnon calls her down to play with BeeBot. Reluctantly, Suzy leaves her drawing to join her teacher on the floor. Mrs. McKinnon shows Suzy the different buttons on BeeBot's back: Forward, Backward, Turn Right, and Turn Left. To program BeeBot to move along the map, she shows Suzy how to press the keys in the right order. Next, she sends the program to BeeBot by pressing the Go button. She tells Suzy to give it a try.

"See, this is a map of a school," Mrs. McKinnon explains, showing Suzy a large square map on the floor illustrating different places like the music room, cafeteria, and library. "Why don't you try to program BeeBot to go to the music room?" Suzy presses the Forward button a few times and then presses Go. She watches BeeBot move straight along the map. "Oh no!" exclaims Suzy. "Why did BeeBot drive to the gym?" Mrs. McKinnon explains that Suzy should look at the map and then program the robot to follow the path. "Imagine that this map is a maze and BeeBot needs to get to the music room to beat the maze," says Mrs. McKinnon. "Does BeeBot need to turn? When? Think about the order and sequence of instructions."

Suddenly, the process of programming makes sense to Suzy. She needs to tell BeeBot, by pressing the buttons on its back, to take a series of ordered steps to get to the music room. She starts by sending one instruction at a time to BeeBot instead of a long, complete program. She can't remember all the needed steps and BeeBot, unlike KIBO, doesn't provide a way for children to see the program they are sending to their robots. With her teacher's help, Suzy tries out a few different strategies for problem solving, such as breaking down the large task into simpler, manageable units by just programming BeeBot to take one or two steps at a time. Eventually, she gets BeeBot to the music room. "BeeBot made it!" Suzy squeals with delight. Her joy of solving mazes has come to life with this colorful robot and she spends her choice time navigating along the different floor maps that come with BeeBot. The next day, when Mrs. McKinnon invites her to play with BeeBot again, Suzy refuses: "I already did all the mazes." So, Mrs. McKinnon encourages her to design her own BeeBot floor maze for herself and her classmates to solve.

A Drawing Turtle

Cindy is a kindergartener who is just beginning to spell and write basic words. She hasn't had much experience using a computer or keyboard but is excited that she will be visiting the computer lab with her class today. She loves to play games in computer class. At the computer lab, her teacher, Ms. Santos, explains that today they will be learning how to program. "A program is a list of instructions that makes something happen onscreen," she says. Ms. Santos shows them how to program using Kinderlogo. This version of LOGO allows young children to explore programming freely by moving a little graphical "turtle" around the computer screen using letter commands instead of full words. Unlike more complex languages, including other versions of LOGO, Kinderlogo makes it easy for young children who are "prereaders," like Cindy. Instead of spelling and typing out long commands such as "forward," "right," "left," etc., the turtle can move with simple keystrokes. For example, Ms. Santos shows the children that they can press the F key to make the turtle go forward, R to make it turn to the right, and L to make it turn to the left. As the turtle moves around on the screen, it draws a line as if a pen were attached to it. The kids are delighted to see how the turtle can be programmed to draw shapes!

Ms. Santos asks the children to program their own turtles to draw their favorite shapes onscreen. Cindy remembers that pressing the "F" key makes the turtle go forward and pressing "R" makes the turtle turn right, but she has very little experience using a keyboard and has trouble finding the letter keys. She has many problems to solve in order to program her turtle: remembering the correspondence between each key on the keyboard and the actions for the turtle, figuring out the right order to press the keys to create a shape, all while navigating a keyboard of letters when she is still learning the alphabet and how to type. This process proves frustrating for Cindy, who is having trouble finding any key except "F" on the keyboard.

Ms. Santos sees that Cindy is struggling. She sits with her to better understand her frustration. She quickly realizes that Cindy understands the concept of programming and the steps she needs to take, but she has a hard time with the keyboard. She helps Cindy out by putting colorful stickers on the F, L, and R keys so she can find them easily. Now Cindy can focus on sequencing her program in the correct order to create a shape. Cindy wants to draw her favorite shape, a square. First, she draws a straight line and then iteratively adds new ones. She also tries out the different turn commands until she gets it right. She has to stop often to make changes and fix things that do not work. Twice she even decides to start over and make a whole new square. By the end of computer class, she has a square onscreen. "Look! Ms. Santos! Look! I programmed my turtle to draw a square!" Cindy beams with pride as Ms. Santos helps her save a screenshot of her program and the square so that she can print them and take them home. As she hands Cindy the printouts, Ms. Santos reminds her how hard she worked in class today and tells her to make sure she shows her parents the printout of her code, too, not just the final square she made. Cindy nods and says she already has a plan for the next time she gets to use Kinderlogo. "Next time, I'm going to try to program the turtle to draw my whole name." Ms. Santos smiles and challenges her to find the different shapes hidden in the letters of her name.

Sean, Suzy, and Cindy all engaged in computational thinking by using different programming environments. They explored powerful ideas of computational thinking and, most importantly, had fun in the process. They engaged with coding in a playful way. The next chapter will explore the role of play when coding in early childhood.

References

BeeBot Home Page. (n.d). Retrieved November 17, 2016, from www. beebot.us/

Biggs, J. (2013). LightBot teaches computer science with a cute little robot and some symbol based programming. *Tech Crunch*. Retrieved from https://techcrunch.com/2013/06/26/lightbotteachescomputerscience withacutelittlerobotandsomesymbolbasedprogramming/

Daisy the Dinosaur on the App Store. (n.d). Retrieved November 17, 2016, from www.daisythedinosaur.com/

Eaton, K. (2014). Programming apps teach the basics of code. *The New York Times*. Retrieved from www.nytimes.com/2014/08/28/technology/ personaltech/getcrackingonlearningcomputercode.html

Lightbot. (n.d). Retrieved November 17, 2016, from http://lightbot.com/

Maney, K. (2014). Computer programming is a dying art. *Newsweek*. Retrieved from www.newsweek.com/2014/06/06/computerprogramming dyingart252618.html

Shapiro, D. (2015). *Hot seat: The startup CEO guidebook*. New York: O'Reilly Media, Inc.

Vee, A. (2013). Understanding computer programming as a literacy. *Literacy in Composition Studies*, 1(2), 42–64.

Playing With Code

Coding can become playing if it is taught with a playful approach. Research in early childhood has shown how play is a wonderful way for children to learn (Fromberg & Gullo, 1992; Fromberg, 1990; Garvey, 1977). Play has been described as a vehicle for the development of imagination and intelligence, language, social skills, and perceptual motor abilities in young children (Frost, 1992). I propose that when introducing computer science and computational thinking into early childhood education, the approach must be playful. Programming languages can, and must, become playgrounds.

Although there are many academic definitions of play (e.g., Csikszentmihalyi, 1981; Scarlett, 2005; SuttonSmith, 2009), one doesn't need to be a scholar to recognize play. Play is when children are having fun, they are immersed in an activity, they are using their imagination, and they are intrinsically motivated. They do not want to stop what they're doing. Those of us who have taught young children to code with a playground approach have witnessed how they want to keep working hard on their projects, even when it is time to stop for snack. When children play, they learn by doing.

Play enhances language development, social competence, creativity, imagination, and thinking skills (Fromberg & Gullo, 1992). Fromberg (1990) claims that play is the "ultimate integrator of human experience" (p. 223). When children play, they draw upon their past experiences, including things they have done, seen others do, read about, watched on television, or seen through other media. They integrate these experiences into their games and play scenarios, and they express and communicate their fears and feelings. As we observe them playing, we can understand them better.

Coding projects can also become integrators of experiences. Mary, a 5-year-old, uses ScartchJr to make an animation depicting the life cycle of a frog. Stephanie, a 6-year-old emergent writer, makes a game to teach younger children the letters. Xavier, a 6-year-old, after learning about habitats, turns KIBO into a bat that hides from the light. Claire makes her KIBO robot turn its light on and off in a colorful pattern. In each of these examples, children bring their previous knowledge into their coding: math and science, literacy and biology, computer science and robotics.

They are also making projects that can be shared with others. Patient teachers, who observe the process of creating these projects, can learn a lot. The clues for understanding learning are not only revealed in the final computational products. Most of the learning happens throughout the experience of *doing*. The art of teaching is in recognizing this process, naming its different steps, addressing challenges encountered along the way, and providing the needed scaffolds.

When coding is taught with a playful approach, children are not afraid to make mistakes. After all, playing is just that: playing. Sometimes we win and sometimes we lose, although some forms of play do not have winners and losers. In pretend play, for example, everything goes. A box can become a castle and a stick can become a sword. Children can be superheroes and monsters. Pretend play in early childhood enhances the child's capacity for cognitive flexibility and, ultimately, creativity (Russ, 2004; Singer & Singer, 2005).

Csikszentmihalyi, an expert on creativity amongst many other things (1981), describes play as "a subset of life . . . an arrangement in which one can practice behavior without dreading its consequences." Coding with a playground approach offers similar opportunities. It looks different from traditional computer science courses in which students need to solve a challenge under time pressure or find the correct way to answer a prompt. The approach I am proposing in this book welcomes all consequences resulting from trial and error. Everything is a learning experience.

The Theories of Play

Classic child development theorists have tackled the subject of play. Piaget observed three main stages: 1) early to late infancy: nonsymbolic practice games; 2) early childhood: make believe and symbolic games; and 3) late childhood: games with rules (Piaget, 1962). Piaget's developmental scheme is based on changes in structure, rather than content, and reflects changes in how children develop a capacity for symbolic thought (Scarlett, 2005). Programming languages for early childhood introduce the rules of grammar and syntax but support the open nature of make believe games.

Traditional Piagetian theory holds that play, in and of itself, does not necessarily result in the formation of new cognitive structures. Piaget claimed that play was just for pleasure, and while it allowed children to practice things they had previously learned, it did not necessarily result in learning new things. In this Piagetian view, play is a "process reflective of emerging symbolic development, but contributing little to it" (Johnsen & Christie, 1986, p. 51). Other theorists, such as Vygotsky, have a different approach, theorizing that play facilitates cognitive development (Vygotsky, 1966). For Vygotsky, make-believe play could foster the development of symbolic thought and self-regulation (Berk & Meyers, 2013; Vygotsky, 1966; Vygotsky, 1978).

I am not a scholar of play, but after decades of observing children coding with a playground approach, I can point to hundreds of instances in which children learned new things by playing with the different coding instructions embedded in programming blocks. I have seen children learn that in ScratchJr it takes 12 turning rotations to make a character flip around in a full circle, just by adding new programming blocks to see what would happen. Additionally, I have seen them tapping around the screen and discovering they can add new pages to their programs, inadvertently learning how to use the app to tell a multipart story. In my observations, before children finish asking the question, "What does this block do?" they've already added it to their program to find out for themselves.

Sometimes children stumble upon a new command in ScratchJr and try it out on their own. This is usually the case when encountering simple concepts, such as those involved in motion. Other times, it was a teacher or a peer who introduced new ideas. It is often the most complex concepts that are learned this way. For example, in ScratchJr, a complex concept and programming block is messaging. The message-programming block allows characters to interact with each other, as one character will only perform an action when it receives a "message" sent by another character (see Figure 4.1). To help children comprehend this abstract concept, I have observed teachers use tangible analogies that children can relate to: if a child sends a letter to a friend, what does the friend do when they receive it to find out what's inside? They open the envelope, which in turn opens their line of communication. This holds true in messaging with ScratchJr,

Figure 4.1 Illustration of how to use ScratchJr's message-sending blocks in order to make two characters move toward one another and have a conversation. In this example, the Kitten and Dog characters talk to one another. After the Dog moves toward the Kitten (eight steps) and bumps into him, the Kitten says "hi" and sends out the orange message envelope. Next, the Dog receives the orange message and replies "Woof Woof." The result is a perfectly timed out conversation between the two characters.

as children can visualize themselves sending a letter to a friend as they use the blocks for creating conversations and games with their characters.

I have also seen children engaging in imaginative play and storytelling. They take on the role of animals and astronauts and used the ScratchJr Paint Editor to insert their own photos into their programs. They became both characters and directors in their own narratives. I have seen children play "dress up" with their KIBO robots and immerse themselves in an imaginary world just like they might with dolls or stuffed animals. But, unlike with dolls, they were able to program their KIBOs to respond to them with movements and sounds.

When children are provided free range to discover new things on their own, in a playful way, I have observed powerful learning outcomes. I conducted a study of over 200 K–2nd grade students and six educators from schools across the U.S. in which we asked teachers to lead ScratchJr lessons in whatever way they preferred. Then, we asked them to administer a standardized programming assessment, called SolveIts, to their students

(Strawhacker & Bers, 2015; Strawhacker, Lee, & Bers, 2017). These assessments evaluate foundational computational thinking skills such as debugging and reverse engineering. The teachers also completed a survey to identify their unique teaching style. Our research found that the "Formal Authority" teaching style, which is characterized by a concern for correct, acceptable, and standard ways of doing things, was associated with lower scores on almost every question on the student's Solvelts programming assessment. In contrast, the highest scoring students had teachers who exhibited a "Personal Model" style, meaning they taught by example and placed emphasis on a hands-on and playful approach to learning (Strawhacker, Lee, & Bers, in press).

These findings are consistent with research that shows that programs with active play components may be more successful in eliciting improved executive functions or self-regulation (Shaheen, 2014). I have observed wonderful examples of digital play that promotes higher order thinking skills when children were provided with opportunities and tools to code with a playground approach. A recent policy statement released by the American Academy of Pediatrics states that "the higher order thinking skills and executive functions essential for school success, such as task persistence, impulse control, emotion regulation, and creative, flexible thinking, are best taught through unstructured and social (not digital) play, as well as responsive parent—child interactions" (American Academy of Pediatrics, 2016). However, what this approach misses is that any kind of play (digital or not) can foster unstructured, social, and playful interactions.

The Role of the Body

Coding environments that use screens, such as ScratchJr, offer limited possibilities for physical play. However, research suggests that learning through movement or "motor learning" is conducive to better outcomes (Dennison & Dennison, 1986). Seymour Papert, in his book *Mindstorms*, called it "syntonic learning" when referring to the LOGO Turtle that allowed children to use knowledge of their own body to explore geometry (Papert, 1980).

Cognitive scientists use the term "embodied cognition" to describe how an organism's body, motion, and sensory capabilities determine how and what it thinks. For example, George Lakoff and Mark Johnson's work on metaphors shows that humans can understand basic concepts that include spatial orientations such as up, down, front, and back because they can directly experience them from their own bodies (Lakoff & Johnson, 1980).

The surge of new tangible interfaces and smart objects provide new opportunities for coding that welcome the body back into the learning experience. Furthermore, they can support gross motor skills development by engaging children in locomotor play that promotes neural and muscular coordination for healthy growth (Byers & Walker, 1995).

Tools like KIBO were designed to bring the playground into coding by engaging the full range of physical play and the development of fine and gross motor skills. For example, it is customary to see children dancing with their KIBOs, marching alongside them in a robotic parade, and running through the same maze they programmed their KIBOs to navigate. In addition, because they tend to mostly test their KIBOs on the floor (the risk of them falling off the table is too great), children are constantly getting up and down, running around to fetch different robotic parts, and stopping on the way to chat with friends.

When children are programming with others, they are engaging not only in collaboration and team work, but also in social play. This involves the development of social coordination skills and social scripts that are necessary for negotiating, problem solving, sharing, and working within groups (Erickson, 1985; Pellegrini & Smith, 1998; McElwain & Volling, 2005). As we will see later in this book, the playful approach to coding makes use of social games such as Simon Says to teach children about the syntax of programming languages.

In sum, a playground approach to coding brings play into the teaching of computer science and computational thinking. If we believe that early childhood education must acknowledge the importance of play for development, then we must bring everything we know about play to the coding class. Best practices for early childhood education also apply when learning about sequencing and algorithms. Coding experiences can be more like games than challenges, or more like pretend stories than problems to solve. The playfulness of the approach can open doors to those who are marginalized from initiatives that teach programming integrated with traditional STEM subjects. For example, this hands-on, playful, and creative approach may help reach females and minorities who are traditionally underrepresented in technical fields like engineering and computer science (Wittemyer, McAllister, Faulkner, McClard, & Gill, 2014). In early childhood, we cherish the benefits of play. May this be our contribution to making computer science and computational thinking more accessible to all.

References

American Academy of Pediatrics. (2016). Media and young minds. *Pediatrics, 138*(5). doi: 10.1542/peds.2016-2591, 1–8.

Berk, L. E., & Meyers, A. B. (2013). The role of make-believe play in the development of executive function: Status of research and future directions. *American Journal of Play, 6*(1), 98.

Byers, J. A., & Walker, C. (1995). Refining the motor training hypothesis for the evolution of play. *American Naturalist, 146*(1), 25–40.

Csikszentmihalyi, M. (1981). Some paradoxes in the definition of play. In A. T. Cheska (Ed.), *Play as context* (pp. 14–26). West Point, NY: Leisure Press.

Dennison, P. E., & Dennison, G. (1986). *Brain gym: Simple activities for whole brain learning.* Glendale, CA: EduKinesthetics, Inc.

Erickson, R. J. (1985). Play contributes to the full emotional development of the child. *Education, 105,* 261–263.

Fromberg, D. P. (1990). Play issues in early childhood education. In C. Seedfeldt (Ed.), *Continuing issues in early childhood education* (pp. 223–243). Columbus, OH: Merrill.

Fromberg, D. P., & Gullo, D. F. (1992). Perspectives on children. In L. R. Williams & D. P. Fromberg (Eds.), *Encyclopedia of early childhood education* (pp. 191–194). New York: Garland Publishing, Inc.

Frost, J. L. (1992). *Play and playscapes.* Albany, NY: Delmar, G.

Garvey, C. (1977). *Play.* Cambridge, MA: Harvard University Press.

Johnsen, E. P., & Christie, J. F. (1986). Pretend play and logical operations. In K. Blanchard (Ed.), *The many faces of play* (pp. 50–58). Champaign, IL: Human Kinetics.

Lakoff, G., & Johnson, M. (1980). Metaphors we live by Chicago. Chicago University.

McElwain, E. L., & Volling, B. L. (2005). Preschool children's interactions with friends and older siblings: Relationship specificity and joint contributions to problem behaviors. *Journal of Family Psychology, 19,* 486–496.

Papert, S. (1980). *Mindstorms: Children, computers, and powerful ideas.* New York: Basic Books, Inc.

Pellegrini, A., & Smith, P. (1998). Physical activity play: The nature and function of a neglected aspect of play. *Child Development, 69*(3), 577–598.

Piaget, J. (1962). *Play, dreams, and imitation in childhood.* New York: W. W. Norton & Co.

Russ, S. W. (2004). *Play in child development and psychotherapy.* Mahwah, NJ: Earlbaum.

Scarlett, W. G., Naudeau, S., Ponte, I., & Salonius-Pasternak, D. (2005). *Children's play.* Thousand Oaks, CA: Sage Publications.

Shaheen, S. (2014). How child's play impacts executive function—Related behaviors. *Applied Neuropsychology: Child, 3*(3), 182–187.

Singer, D. G., & Singer, J. L. (2005). *Imagination and play in the electronic age.* Cambridge, MA: Harvard University Press.

Strawhacker, A. L., & Bers, M. U. (2015). "I want my robot to look for food": Comparing children's programming comprehension using tangible, graphical, and hybrid user interfaces. *International Journal of Technology and Design Education, 25*(3), 293–319.

Strawhacker, A. L., Lee, M.S.C., & Bers, M. (2017). Teaching tools, teacher's rules: Exploring the impact of teaching styles on young children's programming knowledge in ScratchJr. *The International Journal of Technology and Design Education.* doi: 10.1007/s10798-017-9400-9

SuttonSmith, B. (2009). *The ambiguity of play.* Cambridge, MA: Harvard University Press.

Vygotsky, L. (1966). Play and its role in the mental development of the child. *Soviet Psychology, 5*(3), 6–18.

Vygotsky, L. (1978). *Mind in society: The development of higher psychological processes.* Cambridge, MA: Harvard University Press.

Wittemyer, R., McAllister, B., Faulkner, S., McClard, A., & Gill, K.(2014). *MakeHers: Engaging girls and women in technology through making, creating, and inventing.* (Report No. 1). Retrieved from Intel Corporation, https://www.intel.com/content/dam/www/public/us/en/documents/reports/makers-report-girls-women.pdf

PART

II

Computational Thinking

5 | Thinking About Computational Thinking

Madison is a 7-year-old girl who has been programming with ScratchJr for one year at school and at home. As Madison begins a new project, she plans it aloud, adding new characters and actions as she goes along. Among classmates she declares that she is going to make a basketball game. Her favorite sport is basketball. As she explores the ScratchJr library of available backgrounds, she narrates her design process: "I'm going to have teammates and a crowd cheering and a dragon. I should have it in the gym, but I want to add a snack stand to it." Madison enters the ScratchJr Paint Editor and draws a rectangle in the corner of the gym background, representing the snack stand.

Next, Madison adds nearly ten characters to her project. Some she chooses from the character library; some she draws herself. As she formulates her design she expresses an understanding of the tool: "I want the kitten to pass the ball to the girl. So, I'll have to program the ball to move forward." Clearly, Madison understands that ScratchJr is not magic—the characters have potential to do many things, but will only *actually* do what she *programs* them to do. She is in control and must use the programming blocks in the correct sequence to get the characters to carry out the desired actions.

Later, Madison wants the dragon—which she has colored purple—to dribble the ball, jump, and shoot. This requires knowledge of sequencing and order, cause and effect, and an awareness of the debugging process if the characters do something different than she intended. Madison programs the dragon to move right five times to the basketball hoop, then hop. The basketball's program proves trickier. At first, she programs it to move right then hop in a repeat loop. This results in a rigid motion that does not look like dribbling. "No! I want it to move forward and bounce at the same

Figure 5.1 Illustration of Madison's basketball dribbling programs. She has two programs starting with the Green Flag: 1) the first program makes the ball move forward across the screen, and 2) the second program makes the ball bounce up and down.

time!" Madison exclaims. After several different combinations, she has a breakthrough: "It can do two programs at once! Cool!" She writes two separate programs for the ball, one that tells it to move right, and one that tells it to hop (see Figure 5.1).

Madison has debugged her program and refined her problem-solving skills by separating the ball's actions to create a logical program sequence. The ball is successfully "dribbled" toward the hoop for the dragon's game-winning point. Immediately after, a crowd of animal fans cheer via sound blocks Madison pre-recorded. Madison smiles proudly at her masterpiece.

As Madison was working on her project, she explored powerful ideas such as sequencing, debugging, modularization, and design. These are some of the core concepts of computational thinking. This chapter will focus on the growing literature and initiatives in this area. While most definitions focus on computational thinking as a problem-solving process, the approach I present extends beyond this notion by considering computational thinking as an expressive process. While Madison was solving many problems to make her basketball game, she also was telling a story about how a dragon could dribble a ball while a crowd of animal fans cheered. It was her desire to tell that story about her favorite sport that kept her going when she encountered challenges to solve.

In the 1960s, Alan Perlis, the computer scientist known for his work on ALGOL and one of the founding fathers of the discipline, argued that all college students need to learn programming and the "theory of computation" (Guzdial, 2008; Grover & Pea, 2013; Perlis, 1962). Given that computers back then were as big and obscure as the rooms that held them, this insight was surprising. Although Perlis took a leadership role in molding the then nascent field of computer science into an academic discipline, and it was during his term as president of the Association of Computing Machinery (ACM) that the first ACM Curriculum Committee on Computer Science was established, he strongly believed that everyone would benefit from learning how to program. In his "Epigrams in Programming" (Perlis, 1982), Perlis wrote, "Perhaps if we wrote programs from childhood on, as adults we'd be able to read them." This assertion was based on his belief that "most people find the concept of programming obvious, but the doing impossible."

What Perlis referred to as the "concept of programming" is close to our current understanding of computational thinking. Although Perlis was not a developmental scientist or an early childhood educator, he probably knew that even young children could grasp the concepts of sequencing, patterns, modularity, cause and effect, and problem solving when presented in a way that made sense. At the time, Seymour Papert was busy exploring how to create a programming language that children could use, so the doing would not be impossible, as Perlis had argued.

Computational Thinking as Expression

Building on the knowledge gained while working with Piaget, Papert collaborated with Wally Feurzeig and others to create LOGO. This was the first programming language designed for children and explicitly aimed at helping them think in new, computational ways. The term "computational thinking" grew out of this pioneering work, and it meant both solving problems algorithmically and developing technological fluency (Papert, 1980; Bers, 2010). Children who could think like a computer were children who could use the computer to express themselves in a fluent way.

Papert's choice of the word "fluency" was explicitly aimed at referencing language when thinking about computation. A person fluent in a language can use it to recite a poem, write an academic paper, or socialize at a party. A technologically fluent person can use a computer to make an animation, write a speech, model a simulation, or program a robotic creature. As with learning a second language, fluency takes time to achieve and requires hard work and motivation.

Individuals become technologically fluent when they can use technology to express themselves creatively, in a fluent way, effortlessly and smoothly, as one does with language (Bers, 2008). In the process of using the language of computation (LOGO, ScratchJr, KIBO, or any other programming language), one learns to think in different ways. Seymour Papert's computational thinking involved problem solving, but also the notion of expression. I call this the "computational thinking as expression" metaphor, as opposed to the more traditional "computational thinking as problem solving."

The notion of computational thinking encompasses a broad set of analytic and problem-solving skills, dispositions, habits, and approaches most often used in computer science, but that can serve everyone (Barr & Stephenson, 2011; International Society for Technology Education & The Computer Science Teachers Association, 2011; Lee et al., 2011). In 2006, Jeannette Wing's influential article "Computational Thinking" appeared in the *Communications of the ACM* and caught the attention of many researchers, computer scientists, and educators across the U.S. Wing created quite a stir by arguing that *computational thinking*, a problem-solving skill set rooted in computer science, is a universally applicable skill that should be part of every child's analytical ability (Wing, 2006).

According to Wing (2006), computational thinking is defined as "solving problems, designing systems, and understanding human behavior, by drawing on the concepts fundamental to computer science" (p. 33). Computational thinking includes a range of mental tools that are inherent to the field of computer science, including thinking recursively, using abstraction when figuring out a complex task, and using heuristic reasoning to discover a solution (Wing, 2006).

Computational thinking represents a type of analytical thinking that shares similarities with mathematical thinking (e.g., problem solving), engineering thinking (designing and evaluating processes), and scientific thinking (systematic analysis) (Bers, 2010). While the act of engaging in computational thinking is rooted in computer science, Wing argued that it is pertinent to everyone: "It represents a universally applicable attitude and skill set everyone, not just computer scientists would be eager to learn and use" (Wing, 2006, p. 33). Wing asserts that just as the printing press facilitated the spread of the three Rs, (reading, writing and arithmetic) computers facilitate the spread of computational thinking.

Many researchers and educators have cited this 2006 "call to action" paper, as it urges that computational thinking be taught to pre-college students and non-computer science majors. However, although it brought newfound light to the importance of learning how to code, which was introduced in the early '80s by Seymour Papert, it also limited computational thinking to a problem-solving process that complements mathematical and engineering thinking, obscuring the relevance of expression and communication in the act of programming. Students who learn to code with a playground approach engage in computational thinking as a problem-solving process, but also as an expressive process. They develop a new literacy.

Brennan and Resnick (2012) broke down computational thinking into a three-dimensional framework that comprises *concepts, practices,* and *perspectives.* At a higher level, computational thinking practices refer to techniques applied by humans to express themselves by designing and constructing computation. Not surprisingly, this definition of the term from Papert's disciples brings back the relevance of expression in the process of computer programming.

Although computational thinking has received considerable attention over the past several years, there is little agreement on what a definition for computational thinking might encompass (Allan et al., 2010; Barr & Stephenson, 2011; National Academies of Science, 2010; Grover & Pea, 2013). The importance of computational thinking, regardless of its definition, took center stage in 2010 following a stark report titled "Running on Empty: The Failure to Teach K–12 Computer Science in the Digital Age" (Wilson, Sudol, Stephenson, & Stehlik, 2010). This report revealed very low numbers for women in computing and that more than two-thirds of the country had few computer science courses at the secondary school level.

Since then, public and private organizations, motivated by a shortage of programmers in the industry, began to work on frameworks and initiatives to foster computational thinking and address these issues before college. For example, that same year (in 2010), the International Society for Technology in Education (ISTE) and the Computer Science Teachers Association (CSTA) led a National Science Foundation project entitled "Leveraging Thought Leadership for Computational Thinking in PK–12." One of the activities of this project was setting out to construct a clearer definition of computational thinking to be applied in school curriculum. In addition to summarizing many of the skills introduced by Wing, this project also included a list of attitudes toward dealing with computing problems in the face of complexity and ambiguity (International Society for Technology in Education & Computer Science Teachers Association, 2011).

In 2011, Wing published another article in which she redefined computational thinking as "thought processes involved in formulating problems and their solutions so that the solutions are represented in a form that can be effectively carried out by an information-processing agent" (Wing, 2011). Within the playground approach that I propose, this definition gets tweaked. The goal of the thought processes involved in computational thinking is not necessarily problem formulation, but expression. Problem formulation might be a path to expression, but not the end in itself. Ideas are not problems, and we might want to use the power of computers to share and test our ideas. Wing describes the computational thinker as "an information-processing agent." In contrast, I refer to this thinker as an "expressive agent." This is someone who has the internal and external resources and the required fluency to put those ideas into computational media to share with others.

The "problem solving" and "expression" metaphors for describing computational thinking complement each other. However, when the public discourse is too tilted toward the former, which is seen in initiatives that introduce coding as a series of logic puzzles for students to solve, it is important to counterbalance it with the latter. "If you have kids put blocks together to solve the puzzle, that can be useful for learning basic computing concepts. But we think it's missing an important part of what's exciting about coding. If you present just logic puzzles, it's like teaching them writing by only teaching grammar and punctuation," says Mitchel Resnick in an interview (Kamenetz, 2015). In terms of textual literacy, it would be like only giving children crossword puzzles to solve and expecting them to become fluent writers.

Beyond STEM

Researchers, practitioners, funding institutions, and policy makers have traditionally associated computer programming and computational thinking with problem solving. Thus, translated into the educational curriculum, computer science is grouped with science, technology, engineering, and math: STEM. In STEM education programs, computational thinking is defined as a set of cognitive skills for identifying patterns, breaking apart complex problems into smaller steps, organizing and creating a series of steps to provide solutions, and building a representation of data through simulations (Barr & Stephenson, 2011). This traditional approach doesn't allow room for integrating the tools of mind associated with language and expression; it ignores that coding is a literacy. Furthermore, it forgets the work of the many researchers who have proposed that learning a programming language may also be closely related to literacy, akin to acquiring a new foreign language (Papert, 1980; National Research Council, 2010; Solomon, 2005).

The approach I present in this book treats computational thinking as a means of expression and communication. In previous work, I have shown that conceptualizing coding as literacy, and correspondingly using strategies typically used to teach a new language, leads to positive learning outcomes regarding sequencing, a foundational skill for literacy (Kazakoff & Bers, 2011; Kazakoff, Sullivan, & Bers, 2013; Kazakoff & Bers, 2014). For example, we found that children in pre-kindergarten had significant increases in their picture story sequencing skills after completing just a one-week robotics and programming curriculum (Kazakoff, Sullivan, & Bers, 2013). Currently, I am exploring through fMRI techniques the hypothesis that engaging in programming activities has similarities to engaging in language comprehension and production (Bers & Fedorenko, 2016). We are aiming to understand the cognitive and neural basis of learning computer science and developing computational thinking.

To date, there is a lack of research looking at this interdisciplinary issue. Our nation is moving forward with policy decisions regarding the introduction of computer science in education, but we lack the basic data that will provide the evidence needed to make informed choices. For example, as of the date of writing this book, 17 states and the District of Columbia have policies in place that allow computer science to count as a mathematics or science credit in high schools—and that number is on the rise—and other states, such as Texas, approved legislation that allows computer science to fulfill a foreign language requirement, and Kentucky and New Mexico are considering a similar approach. Basic research must inform the debate about the role of computer science in school curriculum.

While the community struggles to come up with a curricular approach and an encompassing definition of computational thinking, ISTE, Code.org, and other organizations have released their own definitions and suggested frameworks for teaching computational thinking. In a recent development, a major collaboration was formed between the Association for Computing Machinery (ACM), Computer Science Teachers Association (CSTA), Code. org, the Cyber Innovation Center (CIC), the National Math and Science Initiative (NMSI), more than 100 advisors within the computing community (i.e., higher education faculty, researchers, K–12 teachers, etc.), several states and large school districts, technology companies, and other organizations in order to develop conceptual guidelines for states and districts creating a K–12 pathway in computer science and computational thinking (A framework for K–12 CS, https://k12cs.org/). The jury is still out regarding the balance between the metaphors of problem solving and expression in this effort.

Computational Thinking and Coding

Computing professionals and educators have the responsibility to make computation available to thinkers of all disciplines (Guzdial, 2008). This responsibility could be easily tackled if the linkage to language and expression were greater than it currently is. Furthermore, over the past few years, there has been growing enthusiasm about integrating STEM with the arts. The STEAM (Science, Technology, Engineering, Arts, and Mathematics) movement was originally spearheaded by the Rhode Island School of Design (RISD) but is now widely adopted by schools, businesses, and individuals (STEM to STEAM, 2016; Yakman, 2008). Adding the Arts to STEM-based subjects, such as computer programming and engineering, may enhance student learning by infusing opportunities for creativity and innovation (Robelen, 2011). Furthermore, STEAM represents more than just the visual arts; it includes a broad spectrum of the humanities, including the liberal arts, language arts, social studies, music, culture, and more (Maguth, 2012).

Research shows that there are many everyday "non-academic" examples of exercising computational thinking skills (Wing, 2008 ; Yadav, 2011). These everyday activities draw on the same type of problem solving inherent in computer science troubleshooting, but do not involve programming. Wing (2008) presents a series of examples, including: sorting Legos (using the concept of "hashing" to sort by color, shape, and size), cooking a meal (using "parallel processing" to manage cooking different types of food at different temperatures for different amounts of time), and looking up a name in an alphabetical list (linear: starting at the beginning of the list; binary: starting at the middle of the list).

This low-tech or unplugged approach to computational thinking is growing. Many people claim that, when working with young children, it is not necessary to engage them in coding, as computational thinking can be achieved through other activities that involve sequencing and problem solving (e.g., Bell, Witten, & Fellows, 1998). I do not agree with this perspective. If computational thinking is to be defined not only as a process of problem solving, but as a process of expression and creation, we need to provide tools that enable the creation of an external artifact. We need a language for expression. Programming languages are the tools for computational thinking. In contrast to most other tools, programming languages provide instant feedback and guide us when troubleshooting and debugging, which is essential in computational thinking.

However, the teaching of programming languages can be complemented by other strategies and activities that in early childhood can serve as precursors. As we will see in Chapter 12, we have developed curricula that take advantage of many low-tech materials as well as singing, acting, drawing, etc. to engage children in computational thinking. Despite this, I strongly believe that, at any age, if we want to engage children in the full potential of computational thinking, we must also provide them with opportunities to code. Can we think in textual ways without knowing how to read or write? Can we be literate without those skills? I don't think so. We must start in early childhood, just like we did with reading and writing.

I have devoted my academic career to understanding coding as literacy and therefore thinking about how to design playground-style experiences that are developmentally appropriate for young children. Through my research at the DevTech research group, we have shown that learning to program with tools like KIBO and ScratchJr allows young children to practice sequencing, logical reasoning, and problem solving (Kazakoff, Sullivan, & Bers, 2013; Portelance & Bers, 2015; Sullivan & Bers, 2015). We have seen that beginning in pre-kindergarten, learning to program a robot significantly improves a child's ability to logically sequence picture stories (Kazakoff, Sullivan, & Bers, 2013). Our findings are consistent with other research that shows the positive effect that learning computer programming and computational thinking can have on other skills such as reflectivity, divergent thinking, cognitive, social, and emotional development (Clements & Gullo, 1984; Clements & Meredith, 1992; Flannery & Bers, 2013).

Coding in the playground is possible and can promote computational thinking. However, the approach to designing the programming languages (see Chapter 11) and the learning environments (see Chapter 12) needs to be developmentally appropriate. The playground approach to coding provides opportunities to encounter a complex system of ideas that is logically organized and utilizes abstraction and representation—as well as the skills and habits of mind to put those powerful ideas to use—by making personally meaningful projects. The next chapter will explore those powerful ideas in the early childhood context.

References

A Framework for K-12 Computer Science Education. (2016). *A framework for K12 computer science education.* N.p. Web. 13 July 2016. Retrieved from https://k12cs.org/about/

Allan, W., Coulter, B., Denner, J., Erickson, J., Lee, I., Malyn-Smith, J., & Martin, F. (2010). Computational thinking for youth. White Paper for the National Science Foundation's Innovative Technology Experiences for Students and Teachers (ITEST) Small Working Group on Computational Thinking (CT). Retrieved from: http://stelar.edc.org/sites/stelar.edc.org/files/Computational_Thinking_paper.pdf

Barr, V., & Stephenson, C. (2011). Bringing computational thinking to K-12: What is involved and what is the role of the computer science education community? *ACM Inroads, 2*(1), 48–54.

Bell, T. C., Witten, I. H., & Fellows, M. R. (1998). Computer science unplugged: Off-line activities and games for all ages. *Computer Science Unplugged.*

Bers, M. (2008). *Blocks to robots: Learning with technology in the early childhood classroom*. New York, NY: Teachers College Press.

Bers, M. U. (2010). The tangible K robotics program: Applied computational thinking for young children. *Early Childhood Research and Practice, 12*(2).

Bers, M. U., & Fedorenko. (2016). The cognitive and neural mechanisms of computer programming in young children: Storytelling or solving puzzles?, *NSP Proposal.*

Bers, M. U., Ponte, I., Juelich, K., Viera, A., & Schenker, J. (2002). Teachers as designers: Integrating robotics in early childhood education information technology in childhood education. In *AACE* (123–145).

Brennan, K., & Resnick, M. (2012). New frameworks for studying and assessing the development of computational thinking. *Proceedings of the 2012 annual meeting of the American Educational Research Association,* Vancouver, Canada.

Cejka, E., Rogers, C., & Portsmore, M. (2006). Kindergarten robotics: Using robotics to motivate math, science, and engineering literacy in elementary school. *International Journal of Engineering Education, 22*(4), 711–722.

Clements, D. H., & Gullo, D. F. (1984). Effects of computer programming on young children's cognition. *Journal of Educational Psychology, 76*(6), 1051–1058. doi: 10.1037/0022-0663.76.6.1051

Clements, D. H., & Meredith, J. S. (1992). *Research on logo: Effects and efficacy*. Retrieved from http://el.media.mit.edu/logo-foundation/pubs/papers/research_logo.html

Flannery, L. P., & Bers, M. U. (2013). Let's dance the "robot hokey-pokey!": Children's programming approaches and achievement throughout early cognitive development. *Journal of Research on Technology in Education, 46*(1), 81–101.

Grover, S., & Pea, R. (2013). Computational thinking in K–12: a review of the state of the field. *Educational Researcher, 42*(1), 38–43.

Guzdial, M. (2008). Paving the way for computational thinking. *Communications of the ACM, 51*(8), 25–27.

International Society for Technology Education and The Computer Science Teachers Association 2011.

ISTE & Computer Science Teachers Association. (2011). Operational definition of computational thinking for K–12 education.

Kamenetz, A. (2015). *Engage kids with coding by letting them design, create, and tell stories.* Retrieved from https://ww2.kqed.org/mindshift/2015/12/15/engage-kids-with-coding-by-letting-them-design-create-and-tell-stories/

Kazakoff, E. R., & Bers, M.U. (2011). The Impact of Computer Programming on Sequencing Ability in Early Childhood. Paper presented at American Educational Research Association Conference(AERA), 8–12 April, 2011, Louisiana: New Orleans.

Kazakoff, E. R., & Bers, M. U. (2014). Put your robot in, put your robot out: Sequencing through programming robots in early childhood. *Journal of Educational Computing Research, 50*(4), 553–573.

Kazakoff, E., Sullivan, A., & Bers, M. U. (2013). The effect of a classroom-based intensive robotics and programming workshop on sequencing ability in early childhood. *Early Childhood Education Journal, 41*(4), 245–255. doi: 10.1007/s10643-012-0554-5

Lee, I., Martin, F., Denner, J., Coulter, B., Allan, W., Erickson, J., . . . Werner, L. (2011). Computational thinking for youth in practice. *ACM Inroads, 2*, 32–37.

Maguth, B. (2012). In defense of the social studies: Social studies programs in STEM education. *Social Studies Research and Practice, 7*(2), 84.

National Academies of Science. (2010). *Report of a workshop on the scope and nature of computational thinking.* Washington, DC: National Academies Press.

National Research Council (US). (2010). *Report of a workshop on the scope and nature of computational thinking.* Washington, DC: National Academies Press.

Papert, S. (1980). *Mindstorms: Children, computers and powerful ideas.* New York: Basic Books.

Perlis, A. (1962). The computer in the university. In M. Greenberger (Ed.), *Computers and the world of the future* (pp. 180–219). Cambridge, MA: MIT Press.

Perlis, A. J. (1982). Epigrams on programming. *Sig Plan Notices, 17*(9), 7–13.

Perlman, R. (1976). *Using Computer Technology to Provide a Creative Learning Environment for Preschool Children.* MIT Logo Memo #24, Cambridge, MA.

Portelance, D. J., & Bers, M. U. (2015). Code and Tell: Assessing young children's learning of computational thinking using peer video interviews with ScratchJr. In *Proceedings of the 14th International Conference on Interaction Design and Children (IDC '15)*. ACM, Boston, MA, USA.

Resnick, M., & Siegel, D. (2015). A different approach to coding. *Bright/ Medium*.

Robelen, E. W. (2011). STEAM: Experts make case for adding arts to STEM. *Education Week, 31*(13), 8.

Solomon, J. (2005). Programming as a second language. *Learning & Leading with Technology, 32*(4), 34–39.

STEM to STEAM. (2016). Retrieved July 27, 2016, from http://stemtosteam.org/

Sullivan, A., & Bers, M.U. (2015). Robotics in the early childhood classroom: Learning outcomes from an 8-week robotics curriculum in pre-kindergarten through second grade. *International Journal of Technology and Design Education*. Online First.

Wilson, C., Sudol, L. A., Stephenson, C., & Stehlik, M. (2010). *Running on empty: The failure to teach K-12 computer science in the digital age.* New York, NY: The Association for Computing Machinery and the Computer Science Teachers Association.

Wing, J. (2006). Computational thinking. *Communications of the ACM, 49*(3), 33–36.

Wing, J. (2008). Computational Thinking and Thinking About Computing [Powerpoint Slides]. Retrieved from: https://www.cs.cmu.edu/afs/cs/usr/wing/www/talks/ct-and-tc-long.pdf

Wing, J. (2011). *Research notebook: Computational thinking—What and why?* The Link Magazine, Spring. Carnegie Mellon University, Pittsburgh. Retrieved from http://link.cs.cmu.edu/article.php?a=600

Wyeth, P. (2008). How young children learn to program with sensor, action, and logic blocks. *Journal of the Learning Sciences, 17*(4), 517–550.

Yadav, A. (2011). Computational thinking and 21st century problem solving [Powerpoint Slides]. Retrieved from: http://cs4edu.cs.purdue.edu/_media/what-is-ct_edps235.pdf

Yakman, G. (2008). STEAM education: An overview of creating a model of integrative education. In *Pupils' Attitudes Towards Technology (PATT-19) Conference: Research on Technology, Innovation, Design & Engineering Teaching*, Salt Lake City, Utah, USA.

6 | Powerful Ideas in the Early Coding Curriculum

This chapter focuses on the powerful ideas of computational thinking (core content and skills) as well as the habits of mind or practices that a young programmer develops. Seymour Papert coined the term "powerful ideas" to refer to a central concept and skill within a domain (i.e., computer science) that is at once personally useful, interconnected with other disciplines, and has roots in intuitive knowledge that a child has internalized over a long period. Papert claims that powerful ideas afford new ways of thinking, new ways of putting knowledge to use, and new ways of making personal and epistemological connections with other domains of knowledge (Papert, 2000).

While the curriculum might use a particular programming environment, such as ScratchJr or KIBO, the powerful ideas and habits of mind, if they are indeed powerful, should be useful when coding with any language. Furthermore, these ideas can also be encountered when engaging in low-tech or unplugged activities aimed at promoting computational thinking.

Computational thinking involves the ability to abstract from computational instructions to computational behaviors and to identify potential "bugs" (Wing, 2006). The challenge for early childhood education is that powerful ideas need to be defined in a developmentally appropriate way and explored at different levels of depth, in a spiral manner, in the sequence of PreK–2. For example, understanding algorithmic thinking in PreK might focus on sequencing, while in second grade it extends to loops. Children will understand that within a sequence, there are patterns that repeat themselves.

What are the powerful ideas in an early childhood curriculum focused on coding and computational thinking? Inspired by already existing computational thinking curriculum such as the framework and resources for educators launched by Google in 2010 (Google for Education, 2010), the work of Karen Brennan and Mitchel Resnick with Scratch (2012), and my work with KIBO (Sullivan & Bers, 2015) and ScratchJr (Portelance, Strawhacker, & Bers, 2015), I propose the following seven developmentally appropriate powerful ideas for early childhood computer science education: algorithms, modularity, control structures, representation, hardware/software, design process, and debugging. After defining each one, I will present examples of how they integrate into early childhood curricula.

Algorithms

An algorithm is a series of ordered steps taken in a sequence to solve a problem or achieve an end goal. Sequencing is an important skill in early childhood; it is a component of planning and involves putting objects or actions in the correct order. For example, retelling a story in a logical way or ordering numbers in a line is sequencing.

Sequencing skills extend beyond coding and computational thinking. Young children might start by sequencing tasks found in daily life such as brushing their teeth, making a sandwich, or following the classroom schedule. As they grow, they discover that different algorithms might achieve the same result (e.g., different paths lead to school; there are a few ways to tie shoes), but that some algorithms are more effective and efficient than others (e.g., certain paths to school might be faster). They can start to evaluate and compare competing algorithms by looking at measures such as ease of implementation, performance, and storage requirements (e.g., fewer steps involved in tying shoes is better).

Understanding algorithms involves understanding abstraction (i.e., identifying relevant information to define what constitutes a step in the sequence) and representation (i.e., depicting and organizing information in an appropriate form). As children mature and encounter different programming languages, they might discover that some algorithms run in parallel. At this stage, it is possible to untangle the concept of sequence from algorithm, but in early childhood education, there is an advantage in teaching these concepts together.

Modularity

Modularity is breaking down tasks or procedures into simpler, manageable units that can be combined to create a more complex process. In sum, the powerful idea of modularity involves subdividing jobs and engaging in decomposition. In early childhood, decomposition can be taught anytime a complex task needs to be broken down into smaller tasks. For example, having a birthday party involves inviting guests, making food, setting the table, etc. Each of these tasks can be broken down even further: inviting guests involves making invitations, putting the cards in envelopes, putting stamps on each envelope, etc. When coding, understanding modularity facilitates the design and testing of projects, so programmers can focus on one piece at a time. As children grow older, they also discover that different people can work on different parts of a project at the same time and bring all the parts together later. They learn different approaches to make modularization most efficient.

Control Structures

Control structures determine the order (or sequence) in which instructions are followed or executed within an algorithm or program. Children learn about sequential execution in the early years, and later they become familiar with multiple control structures that involve repeat functions, loops, conditionals, events, and nested structures. Loops can be used to repeat patterns of instructions, conditionals to skip instructions, and events to initiate an instruction. (For example, when you click the mouse, x does y.)

To understand control structures, young children need to be familiar with patterns. But, at the same time, learning how to program reinforces the concept of patterns. Different programing languages employ different paradigms for working with patterns: ScratchJr and KIBO implement repetition by using loops, while others, like LOGO, use recursive function calls. As children mature, they start to understand the difference between these paradigms and might learn to combine control structures to support complex execution.

Control structures provide a window into understanding the computational concept of making decisions based on conditions (e.g., variable values, branching, etc.). For example, when children program their KIBOs using the light sensor, they can make a program to detect if there is light, and if there is, then tell the KIBO to keep moving forward. Events provide a way to understand the computational concept of one thing causing another to happen. Cause and effect is widely explored in early childhood and using these kinds of control structures reinforces it.

Representation

Computers store and manipulate data and values in a variety of ways. These data need to be made accessible, which leads us to the concept of representation. Early on, children learn that concepts can be represented by symbols. For example, letters represent sounds, numbers represent quantities, and programming instructions represent behaviors. They also learn that different types of things have different attributes: cats have whiskers, and letters use both upper and lower case forms. They also learn that data types have different functionalities. For example, numbers can be added, and letters can be strung together. Some data types are used to construct models (simulations) that produce information on how a system or object changes over time. These models that imitate real-world processes can be used to make predictions. For example, weather data are used to make simulations and predict when storms will hit.

KIBO and ScratchJr use color to represent different types of instructions. For example, in KIBO, blue is motion, orange is sound, etc. When these blocks are put together they represent a sequence of actions for the robot to perform. As children grow and advance to more complex programming languages, they learn about other data types, such as variables, and realize that programmers can create variables to store values that represent data.

The notion that concepts can be represented using symbols is foundational in early childhood and has strong links to both math and literacy. To code, we first need to understand that programming languages use symbols to represent actions. Understanding programming languages as a formal constructed language designed to communicate instructions (an algorithm) to a machine has strong implications for early literacy, which also involves understanding a representational system.

Hardware/Software

Computing systems need hardware and software to operate. The software provides instructions to the hardware. Some hardware is visible, such as printers, screens, and keyboards, but other hardware is not, such as the internal components of a computer (e.g., the motherboard). Robotic kits like KIBO expose those hidden components. For example, we can see the circuit board through the clear plastic casing in the KIBO body (see Figure 6.1).

Hardware and software work together as a system to accomplish tasks, such as receiving, processing, and sending information. Some hardware is specifically designed to receive, or input, data from the environment (e.g., KIBO sensors) while other hardware is designed to output, or send, data to it (e.g., the KIBO lightbulb). The relationship between hardware and software becomes increasingly important in understanding the ways that components affect a system. Furthermore, young children need to understand

Figure 6.1 The transparent side of the KIBO robot. Through this clear side, children are able to explore the circuit board, wires, batteries, and the other "inner workings" of KIBO.

that hardware is programmed to perform a task and that many devices can be programmed, not just computers. For example, DVRs, cars, and watches are all programmed. Furthermore, robots are a special kind of hardware/software combination that involves an electro-mechanical machine guided by a computer program or electronic circuitry. The word "robot" refers to a wide range of machines, from industrial to humanoid, that can perform autonomous or pre-programmed tasks.

The five powerful ideas from computer science described above, algorithms, modularity, representation, control structures, and hardware/software, are all strongly linked to foundational concepts in early childhood education. These concepts span diverse disciplines such as literacy and math, arts and sciences, engineering, and foreign languages. By offering opportunities for children to engage with these ideas in a developmentally appropriate way while coding, we also facilitate the learning of these disciplines. It is a win-win situation.

There are two other kinds of powerful ideas that have more to do with processes, habits of mind, or practices than concepts: debugging and the design process.

Design Process

A design process is an iterative process used to develop programs and tangible artifacts that involves several steps (Ertas & Jones, 1996). For example, traditionally the engineering design process includes identifying a problem, looking for ideas, and developing solutions, and may also include sharing solutions with others (Eggert, 2010; Ertas & Jones, 1996). The process is notably open-ended in that a problem may have many possible solutions (Mangold & Robinson, 2013).

For working in early childhood, we have adapted the design process and developed a series of steps: ask, imagine, plan, create, test and improve, and share (see Figure 6.2). The design process is a cycle: there's no official starting or ending point. Children can begin at any step, move back and forth between steps, or repeat the cycle over and over.

For example, when programming KIBO to dance the Hokey Pokey, some children may spend a long time in the testing phase, dancing and singing along with their robot until they get their program right. Once they share their program with a friend and receive feedback, they may want

Figure 6.2 The steps of the simplified engineering design process that can be used with young children.

to go back to the testing and improving phase to include a dance step they missed. Others may choose to plan each step of their Hokey Pokey program on paper or in a design journal before testing out any ideas. As children become more familiar with the design process, they become instilled with the ability to iteratively create and refine their work, to give and receive feedback to others, and to improve continually a project based on experimenting and testing. This leads to iterative improvement, involves perseverance, and has strong associations with some aspects of executive functions, such as self-control, planning and prioritizing, and organization. Since the design process is such a core idea, more on it will be explored in Chapter 7.

Debugging

Debugging allows us to fix our programs. It involves systematic analysis and evaluation using skills such as testing, logical thinking, and problem solving in an intentional, iterative step-by-step way. When a code doesn't work as intended, troubleshooting strategies can help. Sometimes the problem is not the software, but the hardware, and other times it is in the connection between the two. For example, when children program KIBO to respond to a noise, they often complain that the robot doesn't work. When checking their programming blocks, all necessary wooden blocks are there. However, when checking the robot, they realize they forgot to attach the sound sensor. They quickly learn to check both hardware and software. Once children understand how to debug their systems, they start to develop common troubleshooting strategies that can be used on a variety of computing systems. As children grow, their understanding of the interconnected parts of a system allows them to follow and create systematic problem-solving processes. Learning how to debug is an important skill that is similar to checking your work in math or editing in literacy. It teaches the powerful lesson that things do not just happen to work on the first try, but that many iterations are usually necessary to get it right.

Papert writes in *Mindstorms*:

> Learning to be a master programmer is learning to become highly skilled at isolating and correcting 'bugs,' the parts that keep the program from working. The question to ask about the program is not whether it is right or wrong, but if it is fixable. If this way of looking at intellectual products were generalized to how the larger culture thinks about knowledge and its acquisition, we all might be less intimidated by our fears of 'being wrong.'
>
> (Papert, 1980, p. 23)

In the coding playground, systematic debugging is part of the fun.

Table 6.1 shows how each of the powerful ideas presented here are related to common topics taught in early childhood education.

We encounter powerful ideas through experiences. In the coding playground, a curriculum of powerful ideas provides thematic freedom to relate computer programming and computational thinking to other academic subjects. This is a spiral curriculum (Bruner, 1960; Bruner, 1975), a teaching approach in which each powerful idea is revisited as children mature, at increasingly sophisticated levels. After a decade and a half of work with young children and coding, my DevTech research group has

Table 6.1 Powerful ideas and early childhood education. This table shows the powerful ideas from computational thinking and how they align with traditional early childhood concepts and skills

Powerful Idea	Related Early Childhood Concepts and Skills
Algorithms	• Sequencing/order (foundational math and literacy skill) • Logical organization
Modularity	• Breaking up a large job into smaller steps • Writing instructions • Following a list of instructions to complete a larger project
Control structures	• Recognizing patterns and repetition • Cause and effect
Representation	• Symbolic representation (i.e., letters represent sounds) • Models
Hardware/Software	• Understanding that "smart" objects don't work by magic (i.e., cars, computers, tablets, etc.) • Recognizing objects that are human-engineered
Design process	• Problem solving • Perseverance • Editing/Revision (i.e., in writing)
Debugging	• Identifying problems (checking your work) • Problem solving • Perseverance

developed curricula that provide opportunities for encountering each of the powerful ideas described earlier in multiple ways. Our curricular units are focused on a unique theme but engage children in exploring all the powerful ideas discussed in this chapter. Some curricula are designed for KIBO, others for ScratchJr (see Figure 6.3).

Figure 6.3 Examples of the range of DevTech curricula that have been developed for KIBO and ScratchJr exploring themes of dance, culture, identity, and more.

A Playground Approach to Coding Curriculum

Each curriculum unit that we develop is organized around the powerful ideas described earlier and engages young children in developing:

- **Concepts** that lead to knowledge. For example, the syntax and semantics of a particular programming language and the function of a language.

- **Skills** that lead to action. For example, a systematic approach in generating and implementing solutions, and exploring multiple possible solutions and strategies for approaching open-ended and often difficult problems. Such skills, which have sometimes been defined as practices, are of general applicability beyond robotics, programming, and computational thinking.

- **Habits of mind** that lead to feelings. For example, productive attitudes toward "failure." These attitudes also help to promote executive functioning skills such as perseverance and emotional regulation. Habits of mind are patterns of behavior that become our default.

- **Ideas** that lead to innovation. The creation of an innovative project to share with others, or a new solution to a shared problem, is the result of an idea. For example, one of the kindergarten classrooms we worked with had a problem with squirrels eating the crops that they had planted, so they created a robotic scarecrow to scare the squirrels away.

Over the years, my DevTech research group has developed curricula that combine engaging, developmentally appropriate play-based early childhood experiences with coding. Each lesson is integrated with STEM, literacy, social sciences, and the arts. The goal is to strengthen the overall early childhood curriculum while introducing computational thinking to foster positive attitudes towards computer science in ways that include girls and boys from a wide variety of ethnic and cultural backgrounds. I invite you to view our free downloadable curriculum units on ScratchJr by visiting www.scratchjr.org and on KIBO by visiting our website (http://ase.tufts. edu/DevTech/). There, you can find teaching resources, curriculum downloads, helpful links, and resources.

Our curriculum has the following characteristics:

- Based on decades of research conducted with young children and programming

- Guided by the Positive Technological Development (PTD) theoretical framework

- Incorporates flexible units designed in a playful, developmentally appropriate way

- Understands coding as a literacy and focuses on expression

- Focuses on themes that are highly relevant for early childhood education

- Integrates computational thinking with other content in early childhood education

- Is well suited for children who are learning formal written language

- Has strong social-emotional and cognitive components, which are well aligned with the early childhood education mission

- Designed for different programming environments, robotic systems, and low-tech, play-based activities

- Is a project-based curriculum, not a problem-based curriculum

- Provides a scope and sequence for PreK–2

- Includes stand-alone units that do not sequentially build upon one another, but that explore different levels of complexity of the seven powerful ideas

Each curriculum unit consists of a minimum of 20 hours and is designed to take place over the course of one intensive week of work (i.e., in a camp setting or during a coding or robotics week at school), or over the course of a few months with one or two sessions per week. In addition, all units utilize low-tech materials such as Legos, blocks, recycled materials, art materials, and other manipulatives, as well as singing, theater, games, and puppetry. Each curriculum contains five to seven lessons organized around the powerful ideas discussed earlier. Each unit includes the following sections:

- **Knowledge & Objectives:** What prior knowledge children should have

- **Materials:** List of all technology and non-technology materials required

- **Vocabulary:** Key words that are explored in the lesson

- **Warm-Up Game/Discussion:** A non-tech game or activity that can be played to introduce new concepts

- **Main Activity:** A main engineering, robotics, or programming activity to be completed individually or with a small group

- **Technology Circle "Share time":** Time to get together as a class to answer questions, share work, and explore ideas

- **Ideas for free- play and extensions:** Tips for extending the concepts introduced through child-directed play

Each curriculum culminates with a final project focused on a given theme that children work on over the course of multiple sessions (see Table 6.2). All thematic units are designed to meet both the Massachusetts *Science*

Table 6.2 Sample KIBO robotics curriculum structure

Lesson topic	Children will be able to . . .
1- Engineering Design Process	• Build a sturdy, non-robotic vehicle • Use the engineering design process to facilitate the creation of their vehicle
2- Robotics	• Describe the components of a KIBO robot • Scan a program onto the KIBO robot using the wooden blocks • Build sturdy robots that move
3- Programming	• Point out or select the appropriate block corresponding to a planned robot action • Connect a series of blocks by fitting the pegs of one block into the hole of the following block • Scan a completed program onto the KIBO robot • Fix the sequence if they see it doesn't work (debugging)
4- Sensors (part 1)	• Use a sound sensor with KIBO • Program with the Wait For Clap Block • Compare and contrast human sense and robot sensors
5- Repeat Loops	• Recognize a situation that requires a looped program • Make a program that loops • Use number parameters to modify the number of times a loop runs
6- Sensors (part 2)	• Use a distance and light sensor with KIBO • Compare and contrast human senses and robot sensors
7- Conditionals	• Connect a light sensor to the robot • Identify a situation that needs a branched program • Make a program that uses a branch
8- Final Project	Children build and program a robot of their own design. The final project can integrate with a variety of themes including. Sample final project curricula include: • *Dances from Around the World* (robotics + music) • *Patterns All Around Us* (robotics + math) • *The Iditarod* (robotics + social studies) • *How Things Move* (robotics + physics)

and *Technology Engineering Curriculum Framework* (Massachusetts Department of Education, 2001) and the *Standards for Technological Literacy* (International Technology and Engineering Education Association, 2007). For example, the *KIBO Dances from Around the World* curriculum culminates with children researching a cultural dance and building, decorating, and programming their robot to perform it. The ScratchJr *Animated Genres* curriculum culminates with children designing, programming, and testing their own playable game prototype. These final projects allow students with varying academic abilities to succeed, and they can be easily scaled to meet the needs of gifted or special education inclusion students (O'Conner, 2000).

The design activities are carefully chosen to be of interest to girls and minority students as these groups are still greatly underrepresented in engineering and technology fields, and are informed by research that identified ways to make the format and content of activities more attractive to girls and marginalized populations (Fisher & Margolis, 2002; Richmond, 2000; Rosser, 1990; Sadler, Coyle, & Schwartz, 2000; Tobin, Roth, & Zimmerman, 2001).

All of our DevTech curriculum units involve coding. Children develop computational thinking through coding, alongside other unplugged, low-tech activities. The next chapter addresses the coding process itself and what young children can gain when provided with opportunities to encounter computer science while coding in a playful way.

References

Bers, M. (2008). *Blocks to robots: Learning with technology in the early childhood classroom.* New York, NY: Teachers College Press.

Brennan, K., & Resnick, M. (2012). New frameworks for studying and assessing the development of computational thinking. In *Proceedings of the 2012 Annual Meeting of the American Educational Research Association*, April, Vancouver, Canada (pp. 1–25).

Bruner, J. (1960). *The Process of education.* Cambridge, MA: Harvard University Press.

Bruner, J. S. (1975). Entry into early language: A spiral curriculum: The Charles Gittins memorial lecture delivered at the University College of Swansea on March 13, 1975. University College of Swansea.

Eggert, R. (2010). *Engineering design* (2nd ed.). Meridian, Idaho: High Peak Press.

Ertas, A., & Jones, J. (1996). *The engineering design process* (2nd ed.). New York, NY: John Wiley & Sons, Inc.

Fisher, A., & Margolis, J. (2002). Unlocking the clubhouse: The Carnegie Mellon experience. *ACM SIGCSE Bulletin, 34*(2), 79–83.

Google for Education. (2010). *Exploring computational thinking.* Retrieved from www.google.com/edu/resources/programs/exploring-computational-thinking/index.html#!home

International Technology and Engineering Education Association. (2007). *Standards for technological literacy.* Retrieved from www.iteea.org/67767.aspx

Mangold, J., & Robinson, S. (2013). The engineering design process as a problem solving and learning tool in K-12 classrooms. Published in the *proceedings of the 120th ASEE Annual Conference and Exposition.* Georgia World Congress Center, Atlanta, GA, USA.

Massachusetts Department of Education. (2001). *Massachusetts science and technology/engineering curriculum framework.* Malden, MA: Massachusetts Department of Education.

National Governors Association Center for Best Practices, & Council of Chief State School Officers. (2010). *Common core state standards.* Washington DC: National Governors Association Center for Best Practices, Council of Chief State School Officers.

O'Conner, B. (2000). Using the design process to enable primary aged children with severe emotional and behavioural difficulties (EBD) to communicate more effectively. *The Journal of Design and Technology Education, 5*(3), 197–201.

Papert, S. (2000). *What's the big idea? Toward a pedagogy of idea power.* IBM Systems Journal, 39(3.4), 720–729.

Portelance, D. J., Strawhacker, A. L., & Bers, M. U. (2015). Constructing the ScratchJr programming language in the early childhood classroom. *International Journal of Technology and Design Education, 29*(4), 1–16.

Richmond, G. (2000). Exploring the complexities of group work in science class: A cautionary tale of voice and equitable access to resources for learning. *Journal of Women and Minorities in Science and Engineering,* 6(4), 295–311.

Rosser, S. V. (1990). *Female-friendly science: Applying women's studies methods and theories to attract students.* London: Pergamon.

Sadler, P. M., Coyle, H. P., & Schwartz, M. (2000). Engineering competitions in the middle school classroom: Key elements in developing effective design challenges. *The Journal of the Learning Sciences, 9*(3), 299–327.

Sullivan, A., & Bers, M. U. (2015). Robotics in the early childhood classroom: Learning outcomes from an 8-week robotics curriculum in pre-kindergarten through second grade. *International Journal of Technology and Design Education.* Online First.

Tobin, K., Roth, W. M., & Zimmermann, A. (2001). Learning to teach science in urban schools. *Journal of Research in Science Teaching, 38*(8), 941–964.

Wing, J. M. (2006). Computational thinking. *Communications of the ACM, 49*(3), 33–35.

The Coding Process

Jamie is working on a KIBO robot that will help her clean her room. Jamie, who is 5 years old, has a messy room; toys are everywhere on the floor. She doesn't like it when her mom makes her clean her room, so she **asks** herself: how can I make KIBO help me? She then goes on to **imagine** different ways this could happen. For example, she could program KIBO to beep every time it runs into a toy on the floor to alert her to pick it up. Or, even better, she could build a plow out of Legos and attach it to KIBO and somehow program it to pick up the toys. Or she could just have KIBO running around randomly pushing to the side any toys it encounters.

There are so many possibilities, and some are more complex than others. Jamie needs to make a **plan** and choose an approach. She takes some time to decide and, finally, she goes for a combination of her ideas: she will make her KIBO always go forward and turn right on an infinite loop and, when it encounters an object that blocks its light sensor, it will beep. Then she will attach a giant plow to KIBO's front, and manipulate it to pick up the toy.

Now the fun part starts. Jamie is ready to **create** her project. As she starts working on it, she encounters many challenges. Sometimes she is able to solve them on her own; other times they are so difficult that she chooses to change her plan. As she programs KIBO and builds her plow, she **tests** it along the way. There is always something to **improve**. She doesn't give up. She really wants her project to work. After spending almost one hour on her KIBO cleaning robot, she decides that it is ready and calls her mom. She wants to **share** the product of such hard work.

Jamie's mom is amazed. She watches as Jamie's cleaning KIBO robot travels through the room, running into both furniture and toys, stopping sometimes and others not, beeping sometimes and others not, and getting

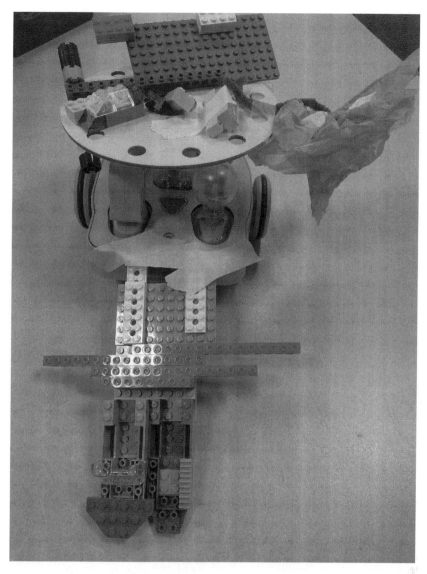

Figure 7.1 Jamie's cleaning KIBO robot. She designed KIBO to travel
through the room, cleaning items up by pushing them out of the
way with the LEGO plow.

stuck under socks and clothes on the floor (see Figure 7.1). She also
watches as Jamie runs behind KIBO, with a LEGO construction (the "plow,"
explains Jamie), bending down and picking up the toys that KIBO chooses
to stop and beep on. Jamie's mom can't believe the amount of time and the

quality of thought her daughter put into this project. It was certainly more time-consuming than just picking up the toys, but Jamie's mom is proud of her daughter. She knows that this is not about judging KIBO's performance as a cleaner, but about supporting her daughter's creativity.

As Jamie worked on her project, she went through the six steps of the design process that we have identified as developmentally appropriate for young children: asking questions, imagining solutions, planning a project to address the solution, creating a prototype, testing and improving it, and sharing it with others. Although Jamie seemed to follow each step in a sequential, organized way, her process was messy. She moved back and forth between steps, she asked new questions while testing, and she imagined new solutions as she was making her robot.

This chapter describes the design process involved in programming. It starts with a question that gives birth to an idea and ends with creating a final project that can be shared with others. The design process makes computational thinking visible: coding becomes a tool of expression and communication. When coding happens while working with robotics, as in Jamie's story, the design process shares similarities with the engineering design process. Starting in kindergarten, every child in the U.S. is supposed to be learning about this, according to state and national frameworks (e.g., ISTE Student Standards, 2016; Massachusetts Department of Elementary and Secondary Education, 2016). My friends at the Tufts University Center for Educational Engineering Outreach (CEEO) have been pioneers in bringing these ideas into the world and are dedicated to improving engineering in K–16 (http://ceeo.tufts.edu/). Through collaboration with a number of companies, such as LEGO®, the CEEO also works to create educational engineering tools. Their focus is on researching how kids and adults learn and apply engineering design concepts and processes. In 2003, my colleagues at the Boston Museum of Science launched the nationwide Engineering is Elementary project (www.eie.org/) and they have been very successful at spreading knowledge and creative resources for teachers interested in bringing engineering design into their schools.

The engineering design process is a methodical series of steps that engineers use when creating functional products and processes. The process is highly iterative and steps often need to be repeated many times before moving on. Furthermore, at each stage there are decisions to make, challenges to solve, and frustrations to manage. This process has been adapted here for K–2 learners and condensed into eight steps. For example, the Massachusetts frameworks identify the following steps: 1) identify the need or problem; 2) research the need or problem; 3) develop possible solutions; 4) select the best possible solutions; 5) construct a prototype; 6) test and evaluate the solutions; 7) communicate the solutions; and 8) redesign. As we have seen in the previous chapter, my DevTech research group has further revised the process to make it developmentally appropriate for children. We only include six steps that are easy for young children to remember and that start with asking a question, not necessarily identifying a problem: 1) ask; 2) imagine; 3) plan; 4) create; 5) test and improve; and 6) share.

Like the engineering design process, the computational design process gives students another tool for systematic thinking. However, the major difference is the purpose of the activity. While the engineering process focuses on problem solving and solutions (i.e., the first step involves identifying a problem and one of the last steps is communicating a solution), the process involved in the "coding as literacy" process starts with imagination and curiosity (i.e., asking a question) and culminates with pride and ownership of the work in a community context (i.e., sharing).

The computational design process (like the engineering design process, the scientific method, and the writing process) introduces students to several orderly steps. However, although there is a sequence, each step is interrelated with the others, such that one is likely to go back and forth between steps. Designing is a messy activity, and while design processes provide frameworks for organizing activities, they are not always neatly followed in practice.

However, all those processes begin with existing knowledge (content knowledge in the case of science, or knowledge about a need or problem in the case of engineering), and gradually become more specific in the search for *additional knowledge* (in the case of science) or a *solution* (in the case of engineering) or a *project* (in the case of computer science). Similarly, the writing process also starts with existing knowledge (our ideas or data on a piece of paper) and gradually becomes more specific as we write, rewrite, and edit drafts in iterative ways, culminating in a final work to share with a reader (see Figure 7.2).

Often, when giving a talk about the similarities between these processes, which have in common the need for background knowledge and skills, creativity, productivity, iteration, and communication, listeners make

Learning through Design

The scientific method
The writing method

Figure 7.2 Illustration of how the design process overlaps with the scientific method and the writing process. The design process starts with existing knowledge and questions and seeks to build and improve designs. Similarly, the scientific method and the writing process follow the same approach in terms of building on what we know to create and improve something new.

connections to a process they use in their own daily work. For example, when discussing with entrepreneurs, many of them show me the similarities of this approach to creating a business plan; when chatting with marketing experts, they often share their experiences creating a marketing strategy. Educators find similarities with the process of developing curriculum and, of course, software developers with writing code. Architects, landscapers, artists, writers, performers, composers, contractors, mechanics: these professionals, who are in the business of making things, go through a design process.

We live in a world made of things. Thus, the process of making those things is of crucial importance and needs to be explored in early childhood. My colleague and collaborator in the ScratchJr project, Mitchel Resnick, writes,

There is a constant interplay between making new things in the world and making new ideas in your head. As you make new things, and get feedback from others (and from yourself), you can revise, modify, and improve your ideas. And based on these new ideas, you are inspired to make new things. The process goes on and on, with making and learning reinforcing one another in a never ending spiral. This spiral is at the heart of the kindergarten approach to learning—and the creative process. As children create towers with blocks and pictures with finger paint, they get ideas for new towers and new pictures. And, over time, they develop intuitions about the creative process itself.

(Resnick, 2001, p. 3)

Resnick calls this process the "creative thinking spiral" (Resnick, 2008), an iterative process that cyclically reinforces creative thinking. As the other process discussed earlier, Rensick also identifies different steps (i.e., imagine, create, play, share, and reflect), but emphasizes playfulness along with problem solving. As children experience the creative thinking spiral, they learn to develop their own ideas, try them out, test the boundaries, experiment with alternatives, and communicate their products.

Young Designers

Little children have big ideas. These are often hard to tackle on a project they can complete on their own, which poses a challenge. On the one hand, we want to help them follow their ideas and ask big questions, but we do not want them to become frustrated when they realize (at the planning step) that they need to trim the ideas down into a manageable piece of work. On the other hand, we do not want to hinder their creativity, nor protect them from failure. We learn from failure, and we learn from iteration.

In solving this challenge, the core ideas of the design process come in handy. We work with children to identify a question or problem they can easily describe using succinct language. We engage them in doing research to understand the big question and the small questions associated with it. We brainstorm different potential ways to address the question, and we help them evaluate pros and cons. We guide them in choosing the most feasible possible solution, and we encourage them to plan how to implement it.

Planning doesn't come easy for most young children, so we use different tools, such as design journals or peer-interviews, to guide them through. We provide them with tools to make a prototype. Once it is done, children test it themselves. We encourage them to get out of their comfort zone and test it with others, as well. This always reveals new problems to solve, as others explore and play with the prototype in a different way than the child who created it in the first place. Children find many problems with these first prototypes, and we provide the time, space, resources, and support needed to refine them. We cherish multiple iterations of problem solving based on feedback. Finally, they feel it is ready to be shared with others. It was hard work. Learning is hard.

Alan Kay, a pioneer in the development of the personal computer, coined the phrase "hard fun" to describe an activity that engages us because it is both enjoyable and challenging. In the coding playground, we provide opportunities for children to have "hard fun," and we support the management of frustration. These are very young children, some of whom are still in the "tantrum stage." Some teachers set up a culture in which succeeding the first time is a rarity and a sign that the child did not challenge himself or herself enough. Others remind students that a project will fail a hundred times before it works, thus anticipating the inevitable. This creates a safe learning environment. It happens to everyone; we learn from failure. Some of the best teachers I have seen over the years invite laughter over failure; just as children laugh at their mistakes on the playground, they can find silliness in their mistakes in the classroom. Having fun and setting up an environment in which laughter is commonly heard is, in my experience, one of the best ways to help children manage frustration when working with technology (Bers, 2008).

Tools for Designers

How do we scaffold the design process for young children? Over the years, my DevTech research group has developed different strategies to guide children through the different steps. However, we must be careful; we do not want to take out the fun of it. Coding is a playground. If the design process becomes too scripted, the playfulness might disappear. We give children a design journal and set up the classroom routine with opportunities to talk about ideas. We reserve time to answer questions about their project's implementation early in the process. We also invite children to interview each other on video about their projects and to discuss challenges they encounter along the way. We engage them in documenting the design process. We sometimes share those videos and materials with parents as part of the child's portfolio.

Design journals, as well as video interviews, make transparent to the children their own thinking as well as the project's evolution. This is also the case for parents and educators. However, children do not always welcome design journals, as they can impose a systematic approach, and some children do not like to plan. Those children might belong to a group of learners that Papert and Turkle have characterized as tinkerers and bricoleurs (Turkle & Papert, 1992), who engage in dialogues and negotiations with the materials as they work with them. Their ideas emerge as they design, build, and program, not beforehand. As Papert and Turkle write, "The bricoleur resembles the painter who stands back between brushstrokes, looks at the canvas, and only after this contemplation, decides what to do next" (Turkle & Papert, 1992, p. 6).

The playground approach to coding supports different learning and designing styles. Some children want, and need, to plan. Others enjoy working bottom-up and messing around with the materials to come up with ideas. Tinkerers and planners complement each other and can also learn from each other. However, there is value in reinforcing the concept of the design process and breaking down the major task of making something. Processes are as important as products. When we ask children to share their projects, we remind them that we want to see their code, not only their final artifacts. We want them to tell us the story of how this product came to be. Just like in any other domain of early childhood education, we want them to show us their work, both the success and the failures encountered in the learning journey.

In my book *Blocks to Robots* (Bers, 2008), I describe how making the design process visible is conducive to "teachable moments," those times in which students share a prototype that is not working or a failed strategy. Teachable moments offer fantastic opportunities for debugging. Debugging, the methodical process of finding and solving bugs, is one of the powerful ideas discussed in Chapter 6.

Learning on Demand

Mario, 7 years old, is working on a ScratchJr game. He created a bunch of flying pigs that make an explosion when they bump into the sun. He is using two pages. On the first page, five pigs are flying in the sky. On the next, there is a bright sun (see Figure 7.3). Mario can't make the pigs go to the next page. During technology circle, he shares his not-working program and explains the problem to his classmates. Immediately, he gets different ideas for how to solve (or "debug") his project.

This approach provides technical information on-demand. It is based on emerging needs of students and presents an alternative for lecture-type introductions. It also fosters a learning community where peer interaction is supported. It supports the development of different roles and forms of participation in the classroom culture. Technology circles can be called as often as every 20 minutes at the beginning of a project, or only once at the end of a day of work, depending on the needs of

Figure 7.3 The first iteration of Mario's ScratchJr program that features five flying pigs. Mario hopes that the pigs will fly from one page to the next to create an explosion once they near the sun, however he has not yet learned the "go to next page" end block yet.

the children and the need of the teacher to introduce new concepts or reinforce old ones.

The challenge with technology circles is that children often ask questions that the teacher is not prepared to answer. This is an opportunity for modeling what programmers do when they do not know the answer. The teacher can first disclose her or his lack of knowledge and say, "Well, I'm not sure. Let's try!" or she can ask the children if someone knows the answer. If neither approach works, the teacher can then assure the children that she or he will find out by asking an expert or checking online, and will bring back the answer next time (Bers, 2008).

Seeking information, solving problems, and learning how to find help and resources are important activities that workers in the information technology industry (and workers in most other professions) do daily. The design process that engages children in the journey from having an idea to sharing a project provides opportunities for modeling useful life-long learning habits. On the way, children develop emotional resources that they can later apply to all domains of life. The next chapter will explore the potential for personal growth when coding.

References

Bers, M. (2008). *Blocks to robots: Learning with technology in the early childhood classroom.* New York, NY: Teachers College Press.

International Society for Technology in Education (ISTE). (2016). *Standards for students.* Retrieved from www.iste.org/standards/standards/for-students-2016

Massachusetts Department of Elementary and Secondary Education. (2016). *2016 Massachusetts science and technology/engineering curriculum framework.* Retrieved from www.doe.mass.edu/frameworks/scitech/2016-04.pdf

Resnick, M. (2001). Lifelong Kindergarten. In *Presentation delivered at the Annual Symposium of the Forum for the Future of Higher Education,* Aspen, Colorado.

Resnick, M. (2007). All I really need to know (about creative thinking) I learned (by studying how children learn) in kindergarten. In *Proceedings* of the 6th ACM SIGCHI Conference on Creativity & Cognition, June (pp. 1–6). ACM.

Resnick, M. (2008). Sowing the seeds for a more creative society. *Learning & Leading with Technology, 35*(4), 18–22.

Turkle, S., & Papert, S. (1992). Epistemological pluralism and the revaluation of the concrete. *Journal of Mathematical Behavior, 11*(1), 3–33.

8 Personal Growth Through Coding

Brandon has been struggling with his KIBO robot for at least 10 minutes. He built a KIBO lion that will run after a gazelle. He saw a documentary last night at home about wildlife in Africa. He is trying to make KIBO move straight forward, but every time he presses the button, KIBO turns. Brandon is perseverant and doesn't want to give up; he is also too proud, and too shy, to ask for help. He wants to do it by himself. He has done it before, when working on another project. He keeps scanning the forward block, but the robot keeps turning. Tom, his best friend, comes over and Brandon shows him the problem. Together they try again, but the KIBO lion doesn't go forward. Tom is puzzled and encourages Brandon to approach the teacher. Brandon is afraid. Mrs. Garcia said many times, "If you don't know how to do something, ask a friend first. Do not come to me." Tom reassures him. They will go together.

Mrs. Garcia smiles, takes a quick look at the robot and points out to the boys the little green dot showing through the clear case of one of the motors, but not the other. Brandon suddenly gets it. Both motors need to have the green dots showing. He thanks the teacher and walks away with his KIBO. Tom is still confused, so Brandon explains to him how the green dots indicate the directionality of the motors. One of the motors was set to move differently than the other, which is why KIBO was turning instead of going straight. Brandon reassembles the motors and this time the KIBO lion works just the way he wants.

Brandon and Tom were doing a lot more than problem solving. They were helping each other, working together, choosing a path of action (i.e., asking the teacher), and supporting each other in their weaknesses. They were displaying empathy and emotional connection to each other.

I developed a framework called Positive Technological Development (PTD) (Bers, 2012) to describe and identify these kinds of positive behaviors through the use of technology: communication, collaboration, community building, content creation, creativity, and choices of conduct. These are the six Cs. Some of the Cs support behaviors that enrich the intrapersonal domain (content creation, creativity, and choices of conduct); others address the interpersonal domain and look at social aspects (communication, collaboration, and community building). These behaviors are associated with personal assets (also using a six Cs labeling model) that have been described by decades of research on positive youth development (PYD) looking at the dynamic relations between individuals and contexts needed for thriving (Lerner, Almerigi, Theokas, & Lerner, 2005) (see Figure 8.1). While the 6 Cs proposed by PYD focus on developmental assets, the 6 Cs of PTD focus on behaviors. Together, these 12 Cs provide a framework for understanding how technology can be designed and used to promote positive behaviors and how, in turn, those behaviors can promote developmental assets. Of course, the learning culture, rituals and values of a classroom will have an impact on how those behaviors get implemented through concrete practices.

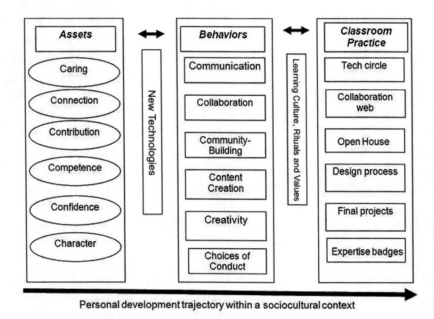

Figure 8.1 The PTD framework, including assets, behaviors, and classroom practices.

PTD is a natural extension of the computer literacy and the techno-logical fluency movements that have influenced the world of education and technology, but it also incorporates psychosocial, civic, and ethical components. PTD examines the developmental tasks of a child growing up in our digital era, and provides a model for designing and evaluating technology-rich youth programs. The explicit end goal of educational programs guided by a PTD framework is not only to teach children how to code or to think in computational ways, but to engage them in positive behaviors. Within the PTD framework, the vision of coding as literacy that empowers individuals empowers individuals can be implemented.

In the PTD framework presented above, context plays a big role. There is nothing in the design of KIBO that prompts children to collaborate with each other. The secret ingredient is in the classroom culture and the curriculum: a setup that favors conversations around small tables and a teacher who invites children to help each other and promotes cooperative activities. It is not the technology, but the learning environment in which that technology is used, that promotes collaboration. For example, if Mrs. Garcia's goal was to promote efficiency and speed in problem solving, she probably would have given children a different instruction than "ask a friend for help before asking me." Mrs. Garcia's goal for her robotics class was to support personal growth. When planning her classroom routines and curriculum, Mrs. Garcia asks herself, "What kind of developmental processes need to be facilitated?"

This question pervades all areas of study: math and science; literacy and social studies; music and movement; coding and engineering. The PTD framework provides a lens to approach these questions in a structured way by using the Cs model. In the next sections I will address each of the 6 Cs as they relate to coding and young children. In each section, I connect a C referring to one of the positive behaviors with a C referring to a positive personal asset: content creation and competence, creativity and confidence, choices of conduct and character, communication and connection, collaboration and caring, and community building and contribution. In total, these 12 Cs form the backbone of the PTD framework.

Content Creation and Competence

The act of coding facilitates content creation. The child becomes a producer, as opposed to a consumer (Bers, 2010a). Brandon learned how to make his KIBO lion move straight forward. But, most importantly, he learned computational ways of thinking and behaving. He learned that he can create the projects he imagines, even if it is hard and he needs to ask for help. A child who can program individual projects is likely to develop a sense of competence and a sense of mastery. And, like a chain reaction, the more competence a child masters, the more the child will be able to do, which sharpens skills and leads to even more competence (Bers, 2012).

When children program, they engage in a series of interrelated steps that might or might not be linear: the design process. They identify a final goal, they formulate an action plan, they make an initial attempt to meet their goals, they test and evaluate, they revise their ideas by assessing what went wrong and what they could do better, and they formulate new attempts to compensate for failure (Bers, 2010a). This iterative design experience may promote and support intentional self-regulation. This set of complex and abstract metacognitive processes is sometimes referred to in the literature as executive functions that enable self-regulated learners to set goals, strategize, and self-monitor in order to process the information around them (Blair, 2002).

Nobel Laureate economist James Heckman (Cunha & Heckman 2007; Heckman & Masterov, 2007) identified skills involved in successful academic performance that are not measured by conventional indices of intellectual ability (e.g., "IQ" tests), as motivation and goal setting, strategic thinking, identifying and recruiting the resources needed for problem solving, and compensating when goals are blocked or when failure occurs. Although there are clearly cognitive components involved in these skills, Heckman and colleagues call these abilities "non-cognitive skills" in order to differentiate them from the specific cognitive abilities measured on conventional mental ability tests. In turn, other scholars have used terms such as "life skills" (Lerner, 2007) or "fundamental pragmatics of life" (Baltes, 1997; Freund & Baltes, 2002) to capture the essence of this set of motivational, cognitive, emotional, behavioral, and social skills.

Competence is not an innate asset; opportunities to create content and become producers of our own artifacts help us gain and reinforce competence. In this book, I make the case that coding is one of such opportunities to master not only powerful ideas of computer science, but also ways of thinking computationally. Within the playground approach to coding that I present in this book, coding means engaging children in making personally meaningful projects while developing new skills. When this happens successfully, we can see children developing a sense of confidence.

Creativity and Confidence

The second C of the PTD framework, creativity, has a strong relationship with the first one, content creation. The act of coding goes beyond using technical skills to solve challenges or puzzles devised by others, as many current initiatives that promote coding have made popular (Resnick & Siegel, 2015). Coding, as a literacy, must support creative expression.

Despite early worries that computers might stifle creativity (Cordes & Miller, 2000; Oppenheimer, 2003), research has found that when used well, programming environments help creativity bloom (Clements & Sarama, 2003; Resnick, 2008, 2006). A creative person can imagine new ways of using the tool of computer programming and grows confident in those new skills. Confidence can be defined as the perception that one can achieve desired goals through one's actions. Confident coders believe in their ability to make the projects they want to make. If they encounter problems along the way (and they surely will), they know they can try many different paths to problem solve. Children who are confident coders have the needed skills to create a project, the ability to find help when necessary, and the perseverance to work hard when faced with technical difficulties.

Researchers have found self-efficacy (or self-efficacy beliefs) to be a necessary component for successfully using technologies to complete tasks (Cassidy & Eachus, 2002; Coffin & MacIntyre, 1999). Competence and confidence often go hand in hand: the more competent someone is, the more likely that person will feel confident. In turn, confidence can reinforce competence.

An important aspect of confidence is the belief that we can improve our skills. Stanford professor Carol Dweck (2006) calls this a "growth mindset," as opposed to a "fixed mindset." Individuals who believe their talents can be developed (through hard work, good strategies, and input from others) have a growth mindset. They tend to achieve more than those with a more fixed mindset (those who believe their talents are innate gifts).

The process of teaching children to code with a playground approach reinforces the growth mindset. Coding invites problem solving and perseverance, and it invites children to ask for help and to give help. It encourages the belief that children can do better in each iteration of their own designs.

Choices of Conduct and Character

The third C in the PTD framework is choices of conduct. The process of making choices builds character. Like the playground, coding experiences can provide the freedom for children to make authentic choices and to experience consequences. In this book I propose that programming languages, among other technologies, can become ethical playgrounds to explore moral identities.

Some of these consequences happen at a micro, individual level. For example, Brandon chose the actions for his KIBO lion (i.e., pursuing the gazelle). Other consequences happen at the macro, social level. Children in a classroom can choose to adhere to the teacher's guidelines regarding projects or can do something else and discover the consequences. Furthermore, we live in a time when we are surrounded by news media about people choosing to use their coding skills in positive or in negative ways, to help or to harm society. There is controversy about hackers and computer scientists like Ed Snowden, who has been called a hero, a whistle-blower, a dissident, a patriot, and a traitor (Bamford, 2014; Gellman, Blake, & Miller, 2013). When one is a competent and confident producer, once has a choice of how to apply those skills. Thus, the C of choices of conduct is truly important to help young children start thinking about ethical and moral choices associated with the power of literacy.

Although young children might not be aware of the complexities of these issues, it is never too early to bring up the fact that coding is a tool, and like any other tool, it can be used for good or bad, just like a hammer that can build but also destroy. When a child first learns how to use a hammer, we explain the precautions that tool requires and we indicate the need to be responsible. The same goes for coding. As a literacy, it is an intellectual tool with tremendous power.

Character is about the actions we take. It implies having a moral purpose and a sense of responsibility (Colby & Damon, 1992; Damon, 1990). Character informs the choices we make, and at the same time, these choices have an impact on our character. This perspective is strongly influenced by Piaget's belief that moral development emerges from action; that is to say, individuals construct their knowledge about morality as a result of interactions with the environment and experiences, rather than pure imitation (Piaget, 1965; Kohlberg, 1973). Morality is not learned by simply internalizing the norms of a group but, rather, by a developmental process that involves personal struggles to arrive at fair solutions and the development of a moral identity (Kohlberg, 1973).

Programming can provide opportunities for young people to explore moral identities (Bers, 2001). Sometimes, these opportunities are carefully planned. For example, I have developed and implemented several projects in which children create robots to represent cherished religious and moral values. Young children and families from Jewish day schools and Catholic schools in the U.S. have explored how robotics can be used to think about not only engineering and computer science, but also moral identities. If you are interested in learning more, I suggest reading about the Mi Ani project in Watertown, MA (Bers, Matas, & Libman, 2013), and the Conciencia project in Buenos Aires, Argentina (Bers & Urrea, 2000).

Communication and Connection

In the playground, there is a lot of talking. Children talk while playing, talk while climbing, and talk while running: the playground is not a quiet place. A silent playground is not a healthy playground. Talking is one of many forms of communication for which the PTD framework advocates. Within this approach, we encourage young children to talk out loud when coding, either to themselves or to others.

When children talk to themselves they are externalizing their ideas and thoughts. When they talk to others they are often sharing a challenge. Research shows that children benefit from these types of peer interactions (Rogoff, 1990). When children talk to one another, they engage in a process of language socialization in which they are learning how to talk and respond to one another (Blum-Kulka & Snow, 2002). Rogoff (1990) highlights Piaget's (1977) argument that children's discussions with adults are less productive for cognitive development than their discussions with their peers. This may be because the superior role of adults might intimidate children from freely expressing their ideas, while conversations with peers can provide the opportunity for reciprocal exchanges, thus promoting the types of social interaction conducive to cognitive development (Blum-Kulka & Snow, 2004). This informs our curricular implementation of technology circle time, to provide scaffolded opportunities for children to talk with each other about their projects.

Communication can be defined as an exchange of data and information. The PTD framework highlights the importance of communication to promote connection between peers or between children and adults. When designing coding experiences with the playground approach, we ask ourselves, "What are the communication mechanisms that will support the formation and sustainment of positive connections?" Activities such as the technology circles provide an answer. Children stop their work, put their projects on the table or floor, and come together to share their learning process. Technology circles present a good opportunity for problem solving as a community. A different method to foster communication that we have used over the years is peer video interviews or "Code and Tell" sessions. In "Code and Tell" sessions, teachers partner students so they can interview one another about their projects, their coding process, and the challenges they faced along the way.

Studies have shown that when playing together at the computer, children speak twice as many words per minute than during other non-technology-related play activities such as play dough and building blocks (New & Cochran, 2007). Research also found that children spend nine times as much time talking to peers while working with computers as they do working on puzzles (Muller & Perlmutter, 1985). How can we leverage these findings when creating coding opportunities for young children? Experiences that effectively provide ways for children to communicate not only facilitate social interaction but also promote language and literacy. This is an essential developmental task for younger children.

Collaboration and Caring

The PTD framework focuses on collaboration to promote caring, defined in this context as the willingness to respond to the needs of other individuals, to assist others, and to use technology as means to help others. Collaboration is a process where two or more people work together to realize their shared goals. This can be challenging in early childhood; however, educational research has found that working in pairs or small groups can have beneficial effects on learning and development, particularly in the early years and primary education (Rogoff, 1990; Topping, 1992; Wood & O'Malley, 1996). Furthermore, research shows that when children are using computers, they are more likely to ask other children for advice and help, even if an adult is present, thus increasing collaboration toward positive socialization (Wartella & Jennings, 2000), and they are also more likely to engage in new forms of collaboration (New & Cochran, 2007). However, for a typically developing young child, the turn-taking, self-control, and self-regulation required to effectively collaborate on a project is difficult. In the past decade, kindergarten teachers in the U.S. have reported that many of their children lack effective self-regulatory skills (Rimm-Kaufman & Pianta, 2000).

Research with young children has shown many ways to foster peer collaborations through coding, particularly when teachers think carefully about the way they design curriculum and how to group children. For example, a recent study conducted in my DevTech research lab showed how young children in second grade could work effectively in pairs to interview one another about their ScratchJr programming projects (Portelance & Bers, 2015). Other research explored the impact of curriculum structure during robotics and coding activities on young children's peer-to-peer collaborations. We found that a less-structured robotics curriculum was more successful for promoting peer interactions (Lee, Sullivan, & Bers, 2013).

To support collaboration, my DevTech research group has developed a low-tech pedagogical tool, called a "collaboration web," to help children become aware of their collaborative patterns (Bers, 2010b). At the beginning of each day of work, along with their design journals and their robotic kits, children are given a personalized printout with their photograph in the center of the page and the photographs and names of all other children in the class arranged in a circle surrounding their own photo. Throughout the day, when the teacher prompts students to do so, each child draws a line from his or her own photo to the photo of the children he or she has collaborated with. For this purpose, collaboration is defined as getting or giving help with a project, programming together, lending or borrowing materials, or working together on a common task. At the end of the week, children write or draw "thank you cards" to the children with whom they have collaborated the most to show they care about them.

Richard Lerner, in his book *The Good Teen*, remembers his grandmother's definition of caring. He recalls her response when showing her his report card: "This is very nice. Getting good grades is important. But what is really important is being a mensch!" (2007, p. 165). This Yiddish word refers to a good person, someone who thinks not only of himself but of others, someone who cares about issues and people outside his immediate world, someone who listens, someone with a "big heart," someone who has compassion.

The PTD framework's goal is to engage children in collaborative endeavors to become mensches. In the process, we promote coding, learning about computer science, developing computational thinking, and learning in general; furthermore, from a positive developmental perspective, the goal of collaboration is to form caring relationships. As the great Jewish scholar and rabbi Abraham Joshua Heschel said: "When I was young, I admired clever people. Now that I am old, I admire kind people" (Heschel, 2017). It is my vision that through coding activities that promote collaboration, we can help young children admire kind people and behave kindly. Fortunately for us, the worldwide community of professional coders also tends to value this. Online groups and collaborative initiatives keep growing and are very active.

Community Building and Contribution

The previously discussed Cs of communication and collaboration support the establishment and sustainment of social relationships when engaging young children in coding experiences. The Cs of community building and contribution take this a step further. They remind us that we must also provide mechanisms for giving back to others, to make our world a better place. Richard Lerner's work shows that when young people are "competent" and "confident," when they have a strong sense of "character" and they can "connect" with and "care" about others, they will also be able to "contribute" to society. All six Cs are interrelated, but according to Lerner, the C of contribution makes them all come together and is "the glue that creates healthy human development" (2007, p. 183). While contribution is an internal asset, a natural capacity of all human beings, coding experiences can facilitate community building.

With young children, community-building techniques may focus on scaffolding support networks that promote each child's contribution to the learning environment (Bers, 2010b). In the spirit of the Reggio Emilia approach (started in municipal infant-toddler centers and preschools of Reggio Emilia, Italy, after World War II), children's projects can be shared with the community via an open house, demonstration day, or exhibition (Rinaldi, 1998). An open house for coding projects provides authentic opportunities for children to share and celebrate the processes and products of their learning with others who are invested in their learning, such as family, friends, and community members.

Teachers may also choose to assign coding projects focused on the idea of societal contribution and community building. This prompts children to make projects with the explicit purpose of contributing to their community. For example, a public school in Somerville, MA, implemented a KIBO robotics curriculum on the theme "Helping at Our School" (Sullivan, 2016). Throughout the curriculum, children learned about robots that perform helpful jobs in the real world (such as hospital robots and robots that clean, like the Roomba, etc.). As a final project, children worked in groups to build and program their own "Helpful KIBO Robots" to do helpful classroom jobs (like pick up trash), teach important ideas, and demonstrate respectful behaviors and school rules (Sullivan, 2016) (see Figure 8.2). As a

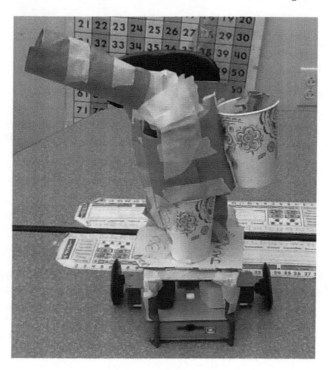

Figure 8.2 Sample "Helpful KIBO Robot." This robot was designed by a child to carry trash that is thrown out through the "trash chute" on top and stored in the paper cups. It is programmed to navigate across the classroom to the garbage and recycling bins in order to help keep the class clean.

literacy, coding can provide the intellectual and material tools so children, as they grow up, fully participate in the ultimate type of community building: the civic society, with its legal and democratic system.

In summary, the 6 Cs of the PTD framework are: content creation, creativity, choices of conduct, communication, collaboration, and community building. These remind us about the positive experiences that children can have while coding, just as they do in the playground. In my DevTech research group, we created a set of PTD cards to help both teachers and researchers implement the 6Cs by guided observations and prompting questions. I enocurgae you to check them out:http://ase.tufts.edu/devtech/PTD.html. The next part of the book will present, in more detail, the two programming languages that I have worked on over so many years: ScratchJr and KIBO. It will also describe both design principles and teaching strategies for bringing coding into early childhood.

References

Abraham Joshua Heschel. (n.d.). BrainyQuote.com. Retrieved May 10, 2017, from BrainyQuote.com Web site www.brainyquote.com/quotes/quotes/a/abrahamjos106291.html

Baltes, P. B. (1997). On the incomplete architecture of human ontogeny: Selection, optimization, and compensation as foundation of developmental theory. *American psychologist, 52*(4), 366–380.

Bamford, J. (2014). Edward Snowden: The untold story. *WIRED Magazine,* August.

Beals, L., & Bers, M. U. (2009). A developmental lens for designing virtual worlds for children and youth. *The International Journal of Learning and Media, 1*(1), 51–65.

Bers, M. (2001). Identity construction environments: Developing personal and moral values through the design of a virtual city. *The Journal of the Learning Sciences, 10*(4), 365–415. NJ: Lawrence Erlbaum Associates, Inc.

Bers, M. U. (2010a). Beyond computer literacy: Supporting youth's positive development through technology. *New Directions for Youth Development, 128,* 13–23.

Bers, M. U. (2010b). The tangible K robotics program: Applied computational thinking for young children. *Early Childhood Research and Practice, 12*(2).

Bers, M. U. (2012). *Designing digital experiences for positive youth development: From playpen to playground.* Cary, NC: Oxford.

Bers, M. U., Matas, J., & Libman, N. (2013). Livnot u'lehibanot, to build and to be built: Making robots in kindergarten to explore Jewish identity. *Diaspora, Indigenous, and Minority Education: Studies of Migration, Integration, Equity, and Cultural Survival, 7*(3), 164–179.

Bers, M. U., & Urrea, C. (2000). Technological prayers: Parents and children exploring robotics and values. In A. Druin & J. Hendler (Eds.), *Robots for kids: Exploring new technologies for learning experiences* (pp. 194–217). New York: Morgan Kaufman.

Biermann, F., & Pattberg, P. (2008). Global environmental governance: Taking stock, moving forward. *Annual Review of Environment and Resources, 33*, 277–294.

Blair, C. (2002). School readiness: Integrating cognition and emotion in a neurobiological conceptualization of children's functioning at school entry. *American Psychologist, 57*(2), 111.

Blum-Kulka, S., & Snow, C. E. (Eds.). (2002). *Talking to adults: The contribution of multiparty discourse to language acquisition.* Mahwah, NJ: Erlbaum.

Cassidy, S., & Eachus, P. (2002). Developing the computer user self-efficacy (CUSE) scale: Investigating the relationship between computer self-efficacy, gender and experience with computers. *Journal of Educational Computing Research, 26*(2), 133–153.

Clements, D., & Sarama, J. (2003). Young children and technology: What does the research say? *Young Children, 58*(6), 34–40.

Coffin, R. J., & MacIntyre, P. D. (1999). Motivational influences on computer-related affective states. *Computers in Human Behavior, 15*(5), 549–569.

Colby, A., & Damon, W. (1992). *Some do care: Contemporary lives of moral commitment.* New York: Free press.

Cordes, C., & E. Miller, eds. (2000). *Fool's Gold: A Critical Look at Computers in Childhood.* College Park, MD: Alliance for Childhood. Retrieved from: http://drupal6.allianceforchildhood.org/fools_gold

Cunha, F., & Heckman, J. (2007). The technology of skill formation. *American Economic Review, 97*(2), 31–47.

Damon, W. (1990). *Moral child: Nurturing children's natural moral growth.* New York: Free Press.

Dweck, C. S. (2006). *Mindset: The new psychology of success.* New York: Random House.

Freund, A. M., & Baltes, P. B. (2002). Life-management strategies of selection, optimization and compensation: Measurement by self-report and construct validity. *Journal of personality and social psychology, 82*(4), 642–662.

Gellman, B., Blake, A., & Miller, G. (2013). Edward Snowden comes forward as source of NSA leaks. *The Washington Post, 6*(9), 13.

Heckman, J. J., & Masterov, D. V. (2007). The productivity argument for investing in young children. *Applied Economic Perspectives and Policy, 29*(3), 446–493.

Kato, H., & Ide, A. (1995, October). Using a game for social setting in a learning environment: AlgoArena—a tool for learning software design. Published in the proccedings of the first international conference on Computer support for collaborative learning (pp. 195–199). Indiana University, Bloomington, Indiana, USA.

Kohlberg, L. (1973). *Continuities in childhood and adult moral development revisited.* Moral Education Research Foundation.

Lee, K., Sullivan, A., & Bers, M. U. (2013). Collaboration by design: Using robotics to foster social interaction in kindergarten. *Computers in the Schools, 30*(3), 271–281.

Lerner, R. M. (2007). *The Good Teen: Rescuing adolescence from the myths of the storm and stress years.* New York, NY: Three Rivers Press.

Lerner, R. M., Almerigi, J., Theokas, C., & Lerner, J. (2005). Positive youth development: A view of the issues. *Journal of Early Adolescence, 25*(1), 10–16.

Monroy-Hernández, A., & Resnick, M. (2008). Empowering kids to create and share programmable media. *Interactions, 15*, 50–53. ACM ID, 1340974.

Muller, A. A., & Perlmutter, M. (1985). Preschool children's problem-solving interactions at computers and jigsaw puzzles. *Journal of Applied Developmental Psychology, 6*, 173–186.

New, R., & Cochran, M. (2007). *Early childhood education: An international encyclopedia* (Vols. 1–4). Westport, CT: Praeger.

Oppenheimer, T. (2003). *The flickering mind: Saving education from the false promise of technology.* New York: Random House.

Piaget, J. (1965). *The child's conception of number.* New York: W. W. Norton & Co.

Piaget, J. (1977). Les operations logiques et la vie sociale. In *Etude sociologique.* Geneva: Libraire Droz.

Portelance, D. J., & Bers, M. U. (2015). Code and tell: Assessing young children's learning of computational thinking using peer video interviews with ScratchJr. In *Proceedings of the 14th International Conference on Interaction Design and Children (IDC '15).* ACM, Boston, MA, USA.

Resnick, M. (2006). Computer as paintbrush: Technology, play, and the creative society. In *Play = Learning: How Play Motivates and Enhances Children's Cognitive and Social-Emotional Growth* (192–208).

Resnick, M. (2008). Sowing the seeds for a more creative society. *Learning & Leading with Technology, 35*(4), 18–22.

Resnick, M., & Siegel, D (2015 Nov 10). A different approach to coding: How kids are making and remaking themselves from Scratch [Web blog post]. *Bright: What's new in education.* Retrieved June 29, 2017 from https://brightreads.com/a-different-approach-to-coding-d679b06d83a

Rimm-Kaufman, S. E., & Pianta, R. C. (2000). An ecological perspective on the transition to kindergarten: A theoretical framework to guide empirical research. *Journal of Applied Developmental Psychology, 21*(5), 491–511.

Rinaldi, C. (1998). Projected curriculum constructed through documentation—Progettazione: An interview with Lella Gandini. In C. Edwards, L. Gandini, & G. Forman (Eds.), *The hundred languages of children: The Reggio Emilia approach—Advanced reflections* (2nd ed., pp. 113–126). Greenwich, CT: Ablex.

Rogoff, B. (1990). *Apprentices in thinking: Cognitive development in a social context.* New York: Oxford.

Roque, R., Kafai, Y., & Fields, D. (2012). From tools to communities: Designs to support online creative collaboration in Scratch. In *Proceedings of the 11th International Conference on Interaction Design and Children* (pp. 220–223). ACM.

Subrahmanyam, K., & Greenfield, P. (2008). Online communication and adolescent relationships. *The Future of Children, 18*(1), 119–146.

Sullivan, A. (2016). *Breaking the STEM stereotype: Investigating the use of robotics to change young children's gender stereotypes about technology & engineering* (Unpublished doctoral dissertation). Tufts University, Medford, MA.

Suzuki, H., & Hiroshi, K. (1997). Identity formation/transformation as the process of collaborative learning through AlgoArena. In R. Hall, N. Miyake, & N. Enyedy (Ed.), *Computer Support for Collaborative Learning '97. Proceedings of The Second International Conference on Computer Support for Collaborative Learning.* December 10–14, 1997. Toronto, Ontario, Canada (280–288).

Suzuki, H., & Kato, H. (1997). Identity formation/transformation as the process of collaborative learning through AlgoArena. *Paper presented at the CSCL '97.*

Topping, K. (1992). Cooperative learning and peer tutoring: An overview. *The Psychologist, 5*(4), 151–157.

Wartella, E. A., & Jennings, N. (2000). Children and computers: New technology—Old concerns. *The Future of Children: Children and Computer Technology, 10*(2), 31–43.

Wood, D., & O'Malley, C. (1996). Collaborative learning between peers: An overview. *Educational Psychology in Practice, 11*(4), 4–9.

New Languages for Young Children

9 | ScratchJr

Lilly is in first grade. She has been using ScratchJr for the last two months during English class. Last week, Mrs. Brown read a story called *Are You My Mother?* by P.D. Eastman. Lilly loved the story of the little bird encountering different animals and asking them if they were her mother. After story time, Mrs. Brown gave children the iPads and invited them to work with a friend to animate the story using ScratchJr. Lilly found her partner, Sam. They loved the idea! They spent some time discussing what scenes they were going to create because they wanted to match the story to the available pages in ScratchJr. They decided to make the bird talk with the dog first, then go to the next page to talk with the cat, and finally the bird would talk with a steam shovel.

While Sam wanted to draw the characters on his own, Lilly wanted to use the iPad to take pictures of the book's drawings and import them into the already existing ScratchJr library. After some back and forth, Sam agreed to this proposal, only if he could use the ScratchJr paint editor to add some stripes to the cat. He thought the book's illustrations needed some spicing up. Once both children agreed on the look of the main characters, it was time to start programming. Lilly wanted the bird to ask the cat, "Are you my mother?" and the cat to respond with a "meow." She set out to put together her ScratchJr program by snapping together the "Say" blocks, which allow characters to express themselves via speech bubbles. When trying out her program, Lilly noticed that the cat and the bird were speaking at the same time, unlike conversations in real life where, according to Lilly, "You're supposed to wait for the other person to talk before you respond." She started tinkering with different blocks until she discovered what she thought was a perfect solution to this problem: she connected a "Wait" block after each "Say" block in her program.

The function of the "Wait" block, which looks like the face of a clock, is to pause the program for a period. The way Lilly placed these blocks into her program caused intervals of time between the characters' speech bubbles. As a result, the conversation between the bird and the cat felt more natural. Sam liked this solution. During whole-class technology circle time, Lilly and Sam were proud to share their project with their classmates. Many other students wanted to know how they got their characters to talk to each other. Beaming, Lilly showed the class the code and carefully explained how she programmed the amount of time that the characters would "wait" before saying their lines. It was a trial and error process. At the end of this activity, Mrs. Brown showed the children how to share their interactive stories with their parents via email so they could see their projects at home.

Lilly and Sam are two children from over 6 million around the world who are learning to code and creating their own interactive stories with the free ScratchJr app. ScratchJr was launched in July 2014 (Bers & Resnick, 2015). From then until March 2016, it was downloaded over 6 million times, and it records an average of over 104,000 worldwide users per week. ScratchJr is used in 191 countries across the globe. As of today, we are proud that ScratchJr can be downloaded to iPads, Android tablets, Amazon Kindle tablets, and Chromebooks, and we are tirelessly working on making the application available on other platforms. Translations in Spanish, Dutch, French, Catalan, Italian, and Thai are also available, and we are actively adding new languages to improve localization. Our goal is to provide a free programming language for every young child to learn to code, to think in new ways, and to use technology for self-expression in a playground style.

The rapid growth and penetration of ScratchJr in early childhood education, such as in Lilly and Sam's first grade classroom, shows that teachers want and need technological playgrounds for young children. While Mrs. Brown did not have time allocated in her day for a computer or programming class, she was able to creatively integrate ScratchJr in her English class. Before ScratchJr, she might have asked children to recreate the *Are You My Mother?* story with crayons and paper. Now, with ScratchJr, she could incorporate coding into this activity. Children engaged with literacy and with programming skills simultaneously. Furthermore, they wove together their creativity and problem solving with their excitement and pride, sharing their projects with peers at school and parents at home.

Like many creative endeavors, ScratchJr started with a question: how can we make a programming language developmentally appropriate for young children? We were inspired by Scratch, designed for children ages 8 and up by Mitch Resnick and his team at the MIT Media Lab, which is used by millions of young people around the world (visit scratch.mit.edu to find out more).

After observing my own three children, who were young at the time, trying to program on their own with Scratch, I realized the need to make some important design changes. They understood the basic programming concepts, but it was hard for them to manipulate the interface. They were lost with the many choices of programming commands that they couldn't read or comprehend. With an adult mediating the experience, they could happily use Scratch, but they could not work on their own. This troubled me. Children do not need an adult to hold their hand at the playground. They can figure out how to use the equipment and how to navigate the social rules. They might need help for the more challenging tasks, but generally speaking, playgrounds are designed so children can play and experiment on their own. I wanted a programming language that would enable the same experience of freedom and exploration and the same sense of mastery, without an adult stewarding every action.

Resnick and I decided to collaborate on the ScratchJr project and brought to our team old friends and colleagues Paula Bonta and Brian Silverman from the Playful Invention Company (PICO) in Canada. The adventure began in 2011 when we received a grant from the National Science Foundation to start the research and design process (NSF 1118664). In addition, we received generous support from the Scratch Foundation, which was developed to provide support and raise funds for the Scratch ecosystem. It took us three years to get ready to launch ScratchJr. We wanted an age-appropriate programming language for children ages 5–7. We wanted a digital playground to create interactive stories and games using graphical blocks. We wanted to do it right. Therefore, we sought out the best design partners available at each stage of development for guidance and valued input, including early childhood educators, parents, principals, and children themselves.

The Tool

ScratchJr is a digital playground for coding. We spent a great amount of time working in partnership with graphic designers so the interface would convey playfulness. The color scheme sets a playful tone, the graphics are bright and whimsical, and the programmable actions are fun. Children drawn to artistic endeavors can design characters and backgrounds. Children drawn to animations can explore the range of programming concepts systematically or by tinkering. Children can snap together graphical programming blocks to make their characters move, jump, dance, and sing. They can modify characters in the paint editor, create colorful backgrounds, add their own voices and sounds, and even take photos of themselves to insert into their stories.

ScratchJr has a user's library of projects, a main project editor, and tools for selecting and drawing characters and background graphics (Figure 9.1). At the center of the project editor is the story page, the scene under construction. New characters, text, and settings can be added by clicking large buttons labeled with icons: a cat silhouette, the letter A, and a mountain range. Pages (thumbnails of which appear on the right-hand side) can be created and played in sequence as multi-scene stories.

The blue palette of programming instructions lies along the center of the editor. Children display one instruction category at a time by clicking selectors on the left. Dragging instruction blocks from the palette into the scripting area below activates them. Snapping blocks together creates programs that are read and played from left to right. The "Green Flag" ("Play")

Figure 9.1 The ScratchJr interface.

and red "Stop" buttons respectively start and interrupt the programmed animation.

The programming blocks are organized into six categories represented by different colors: yellow Trigger blocks, blue Motion blocks, purple Looks blocks, green Sound blocks, orange Control flow blocks, and red End blocks (see Table 9.1).

When put together as a jigsaw puzzle, these programming blocks allow children to control their character's actions on the screen. For example, the following image shows a programming script for a character hopping twice and then growing and shrinking (see Figure 9.2).

The design of the block shapes prevents syntax errors. The jigsaw puzzle pieces have visual properties that correspond to their syntactic properties. For example, the "Repeat Forever" block can only appear at the end of a program. Since nothing should follow a "Repeat Forever" command, the right side of this block is rounded so that another jigsaw piece cannot attach to it (see Figure 9.3).

A programming script runs as a sequence from left to right instead of the traditional top-to-bottom format of most programming languages, including Scratch. This choice reinforces print-awareness and English literacy skills. As a character's script runs, the app highlights each block as it is executed, representing the instructions given to that character on the stage.

When the app opens to the project screen, the Motion blocks are shown within the blocks palette in the middle of the screen (Figure 9.4). Children can drag as many Motion blocks from the palette to the programming area below it and then connect them to create scripts. To program with blocks from other categories, children may tap one of the color-coded buttons on the left side of the palette. For example, if a child taps the purple button, the Motion blocks on the palette are replaced with Looks blocks. In this way, children have access to over 25 programming blocks, without being overwhelmed by options on the screen. Text showing the name of each block can be revealed by tapping it, which supports word recognition.

The programming blocks span concepts from simple sequencing of motion to control structures. Most of the powerful ideas of computer science described in Chapter 6 can be encountered when making a ScratchJr project. In addition, children can use ScratchJr for other activities beyond coding. They can create and modify characters in the paint editor, record their own voices and sounds, and even insert photos of themselves that

Table 9.1 ScratchJr programming block categories. For more detailed descriptions of individual programming blocks see www.scratchjr.org/learn.html

Block Category	Sample Block	Category Description
Triggering blocks	"Start on Green Flag"	These blocks can be placed at the beginning of a script in order to make that script execute when a certain event happens. For example, when the "Start on Green Flag" block is placed at the beginning of a script, the script will execute whenever the green flag at the top right of the screen is tapped.
Motion blocks	"Move Right" (1 step)	These blocks make characters move up, down, left, and right. They can also make characters go back to the place they started, rotate, and hop.
Looks blocks	"Grow"	These blocks change how characters look. This set includes blocks that change the size of the character, add a speech bubble with user-defined text, and show or hide the character.
Sound blocks	"Play Pop"	Sound blocks play a sound in ScratchJr's library. Children can also record a sound and save it in a new Sound block.
Control flow blocks	"Wait" (1/10th second)	Unlike Motion or Looks blocks, which visibly change the characters on the stage, Control flow blocks change the nature of a character's program. For example, a sequence of blocks can go inside of a "Repeat" block and then the user can change the number on this block to determine how many times the given script will execute.
End blocks	"Repeat Forever"	These blocks can be placed at the end of the program and determine whether something happens when the program finishes executing.

Figure 9.2 A script in ScratchJr comprising six programming blocks. This script will start when the user presses the green flag. When the script runs, the corresponding character will hop twice, then grow by two times, and then shrink by two times back to its original size.

Figure 9.3 "Repeat Forever" block with rounded right side.

Figure 9.4 The circled blue Motion blocks are shown within the blocks palette in the middle of the screen.

they take in the paint editor using the camera option. Then they can incorporate those media rich materials into their projects to personalize them. ScratchJr comes with a small basic set of graphics compared to the hundreds available in Scratch. This decision was motivated by our overarching theme that "less is more" to ease children's difficulty in navigating vast arrays of options. Furthermore, it encourages them to create their own new graphics that might relate to classroom-specific themes. Children can edit the included images or draw their own in an embedded scalable vector graphics editor. Data shows that 11 percent of all projects created by children include either a character or background that was created in the Paint Editor. Furthermore, the most common character added in ScratchJr, encompassing 30 percent of the characters added during sessions, is "User Asset," or a character created or altered in some way in the paint editor. This demonstrates users' desire to add personal and unique aspects to their projects.

ScratchJr has a feature called "the grid" that overlays the animation stage (see Figure 9.5). It can be toggled on and off, as is most helpful when used during programming (as opposed to when presenting a project). The grid was designed to help children understand the units of measurement for each programming block. It addresses the countable unit of measurement

Figure 9.5 ScratchJr has a grid feature.

for linear movement. For example, a character programmed to "Move Right 10" glides 10 grid cells rather than 10 pixels or an arbitrary unit.

The grid is similar to the upper right quadrant of the Cartesian coordinate system, with discrete rather than continuous units of measure. Its numbered axes prompt counting and provide a marker to track counting. Children may use several methods to relate the numbers on the axes to the number representing a desired amount of motion along that axis.

Motion created by a single script always parallels either the vertical or horizontal axis, ensuring that the grid-cell unit of measure always corresponds to the distance the character will move. In using the grid, several possible strategies for programming movement of a given distance facilitate exploration of increasingly sophisticated number and programming concepts. For example, to move a character three-grid squares, a child could sequence three "Move 1" blocks, using the default parameter value for this block. The child could also use a single "Move 1" block and click the script or the Play button three times. Finally, the child could change the number parameter, creating a "Move 3" block (see Figure 9.6). The grid's cells and numbered axes allow for strategies varying in complexity, from estimating and adjusting, to counting, to basic arithmetic. The design of the grid was

Figure 9.6 Multiple ways to move Kitten with ScratchJr with blue Motion blocks.

influenced by our goal to facilitate the integration of ScratchJr with other curricular disciplines: in this case, math.

Furthermore, several design decisions were made for seamless integration with literacy. The ability to create up to four independent "pages" and to integrate text and speech into a project allows children to create their own storybooks with a beginning, middle, and end. When creating these projects, children think in terms of "if this happens, then this happens." By programming with ScratchJr, they can begin to understand the basic components of a story while also reinforcing sequencing skills.

While working with ScratchJr, children encounter powerful ideas and develop skills that can be applied across domains, such as sequencing, estimation, prediction, composition, and decomposition. "How many?" or "How far?" are questions commonly heard when children are using ScratchJr. Furthermore, experienced teachers invite children to predict what will happen when they run each iteration of their program, and to think about whether the changes they have made will result in their intended outcome. ScratchJr provides immediate feedback about the accuracy of their estimations and predictions. That is the beauty of a programming language: computational thinking can be tested and feedback received.

Many of ScratchJr's design features support problem solving by reducing unnecessary low-level cognitive burdens, freeing up mental resources for high-level processes such as troubleshooting a script that produces unexpected outcomes. These design decisions keep the challenge at an appropriate level and may help young children devote sufficient cognitive resources to the many high-level thinking processes involved in imagining and creating a program. When the goal of coding is expression, this is much needed.

Our Design Process

We started our design and development process by observing how young children used Scratch, designed for older children, and noting their difficulties. We spent many hours in local kindergarten, first, and second grade classrooms to understand the limitations for our intended age range, 5 to 7 years old (Flannery et al., 2013). For example, we noted that children were getting lost with so many possibilities for programing commands. Thus, we learned early on about the need to simplify and offer a more limited programming palette. We also noticed that movement happened too fast and children had a difficult time understanding the relationship between the programming blocks and their resulting actions. Thus, we decided to slow down processes, so every block would take time before the triggering of the action. Teachers pointed out that, as children were learning how to read and write from left to right, it might be a good idea to mirror this directionality in ScratchJr. In contrast, Scratch is programmed from top to bottom to mimic other established and more advanced programming languages. Based on these findings we started the design of our first ScratchJr prototypes, Alpha and Beta.

Throughout each stage of development, we did user testing with young children, parents, and educators. While this approach might have slowed down the development process, it ensured that we created a programming language that each of these groups, in their diversity of needs and wants, would find useful. We worked with hundreds of teachers and children through informal afterschool sessions, educator workshops, experimental classroom interventions, and at-home play sessions. Additionally, we conducted online surveys and face-to-face focus groups to obtain feedback. These provided valuable insights for our design team.

Alpha, the initial prototype, was web-based. It required children and teachers to log in to a private server. This version addressed our overarching goals of scaling down the Scratch programming environment to appeal to a younger audience (e.g., less text on the screen, more inviting and colorful graphics, large programming blocks with simple commands, etc.). However, the username system was poorly received as teachers had difficulty keeping track of students' login credentials, and students forgot them. Furthermore, most of the children could not type with accuracy anyway. By using the Alpha web-based prototype, most children ended up with multiple accounts and lost their work, while teachers were frustrated because they spent most of their time with the school's technical administration team, rather than focusing on the children learning programming concepts.

Through focus groups and surveys, we heard loud and clear that most teachers wanted to have a ScratchJr version that did not require internet access. Many schools had slow connectivity that caused lags and errors as students worked, creating frustration for both students and teachers. Others did not have connectivity at all. Teachers wanted a stand-alone application. Furthermore, they wanted a tablet version, not a desktop or laptop computer version. It is conceivable that this wish was partially spurred by the growing popularity in 2011 and 2012 of Apple iPad tablets and touch-screen devices, but our research also showed that students had considerable difficulty manipulating mice and touchpads when using ScratchJr on computers.

We released the Beta version of ScratchJr as a tablet interface for iPads, which did show improvements in children's ability to quickly and fluently create projects. However, due to technical issues, classrooms still needed access to wireless internet. We created an experimental Admin Panel, a master-user webpage for teachers that grouped all student accounts and completed work in one location. While there were some successes with this method (for example, it was easy for teachers to view all student work at once), the Admin Panel was overwhelming to use, as each classroom had hundreds of projects by the end of a single unit. Furthermore, log in credentials were still required and problematic.

While our technical team was working on the platform issues, we experimented with different kinds of programming blocks and the grouping of the blocks into categories. Teachers suggested setting the "rotate character" block at 12 steps so it could perform a full rotation. This number corresponds with an analog clock, a topic typically covered in first and second grade. We also explored the different tool options. Children provided extensive feedback on the camera functionality in the paint editor, the sound recording feature in the Sound blocks palette, the colorful highlighting of blocks as they are running within a program, and the drag-to-copy feature that allows characters and their code to be shared across multiple pages in a single project. Parents applauded our decision to have no internet links or "pop-ups" anywhere in the app (so children could not accidentally get online), except for the email-sharing feature to send projects to family members or other devices. The sharing feature has played an important role in fostering a ScratchJr community in which children can share what they have made in school with friends and family at home.

In conjunction with our design team, h24 Creative Studio, we experimented with different looks and metaphors for the interface. For example, Figures 9.7, 9.8, and 9.9 show the different feels of the interfaces we experimented with, from a digital feel to a traditional notebook to a wooden surface.

All along the design process, we struggled with an important decision: the look of the ScratchJr kitten. We explored different ideas until we were all happy (see Figure 9.10).

Figure 9.7 ScratchJr Interface 1 "Digital Feel" design.

Figure 9.8 ScratchJr Interface 2 "Notebook" design.

Figure 9.9 ScratchJr Interface 3 "Wooden" design.

Figure 9.10 The ScratchJr Kitten was influenced by the Scratch Cat, of the Scratch Programming language developed in 2007. The Kitten went through many iterations until the team agreed on what it looks like today.

By July 2014, after a successful Kickstarter campaign to raise funds to complement our already existing grant, we launched the current version of ScratchJr as a native tablet app. We removed the username and admin panel systems and we developed a simple one-to-one-device sharing model.

Projects can now be shared via email or via Apple's AirDrop feature. This was a compromise for school and home use. As creators of ScratchJr, we immersed ourselves in a journey that took us through the different steps of the design process. It was fun.

ScratchJr Today

Since the release of ScratchJr for iPads, teachers around the world started to ask for an Android version, so we expanded our team. At the time, Mark Roth, a managing director and software engineer at Two Sigma Investments, and a proud father of two boys, had just learned of ScratchJr. Disappointed to hear there was no Android version yet, he later approached Resnick to volunteer his spare time with the team. Together with Kevin Hu, another software engineer at Two Sigma, the team released a Beta version in November 2014 and a final version in March 2015. Today, the Android version is officially supported by the Scratch team, works on Android 4.2+ (Jelly Bean or higher) with 7" screens or larger, and has seen over 200,000 downloads (and is growing rapidly).

Mark worked on this project because he believes it is important for people around the world to have access to tools that allow creative minds to explore. He knows that Android is a more common platform outside the U.S., so he decided to help out by volunteering his time. Using the Android version, we then created a version for Amazon tablets in January 2016 and further expanded it by making ScratchJr compatible with Chromebook devices in March 2016. Making ScratchJr available on many different devices has allowed the application to have a more global impact. ScratchJr is actively used in 191 countries worldwide (out of 196), used the most in the U.S., the United Kingdom, Australia, Canada, Sweden, Spain, Finland, South Korea, France, and China.

Furthermore, in December 2015 we launched PBS KIDS ScratchJr, in collaboration with PBS KIDS, so children could create their own interactive stories and games using over 150 characters and backgrounds from popular children's television programs produced by PBS KIDS, such as *Wild Kratts, Wordgirl, Peg + Cat* and *Nature Cat* (www.pbs.org/about/blogs/news/pbs-kids-launches-free-scratchjr-app-helping-young-children-learn-to-code-and-code-to-learn/). The app was developed as part of the Corporation for Public Broadcasting (CPB) and the PBS Ready To Learn Initiative with

129

funding from the U.S. Department of Education and, at the time of writing this book, had over 434,177 downloads.

The ScratchJr team began collecting analytics data in January 2016, which has provided a more comprehensive overview of how children and educators are using the application. Since then, as of December 2016, over 6.8 million projects have been created, and over 8 million existing projects have been opened again and edited, indicating that users are working on improving and altering the same projects over time. Additionally, almost 250,000 projects have been shared with others via email or Apple AirDrop. In this relatively short time span, over 130 million programming blocks have been used, the most popular blocks being "Forward," "Start on Green Flag," "Up," "Backward," and "Say." The "Say" block is used so that characters within a project can communicate with each other—the notion that it is in the top five most used blocks on ScratchJr shows that children are using the app to build upon their storytelling skills. Furthermore, users around the world spend a consistent average of 14 minutes per session creating projects in ScratchJr. Additionally, ScratchJr maintains an 80 percent rate of returning users, while still bringing in a consistent 20 percent rate of new users each month. ScratchJr is certainly growing rapidly, and those who use it keep coming back to program more. By the time you are reading this book, these numbers will have increased.

A Playground on the Screen

Children's projects show the depth of their creativity. A popular kindergarten activity with ScratchJr involves designing and creating collages with embedded animations about their favorite places, activities, or special people in their lives. Children exploring storytelling have used classic storybooks by Eric Carle, Mo Willems, and Maurice Sendak for inspiration, and then programmed their own original multi-page stories. These projects allow children to imagine new endings to favorite tales, or even to invent new narratives of their own. For example, children have created versions of *Little Red Riding Hood* where Little Red and the Wolf became friends, or fantasy stories about dragons and wizards traveling to another planet to save earth. Older children, inspired by game mechanics in mazes, Tetris, and Frogger, delight in building projects that are interactive. Children explore perspective-taking and user-centered design by developing simple interactive games, and testing them out with their friends and family.

ScratchJr provides the opportunity for a digital coding playground. As evidenced by the diversity of experiences described earlier, children can playfully program their own stories, games, and animations. Furthermore, when working on their own, children have chosen to program the artwork they themselves created. This is something that is happening spontaneously in the ScratchJr playground. Children use their imagination and art skills, along with their coding and problem-solving strategies.

ScratchJr is an open-ended programing environment that engages children in the six positive behaviors (6 Cs), proposed by the PTD framework. Thus, it engages children in making their own projects (i.e., *content creation*). Throughout this iterative creation process, children develop computational thinking concepts, skills, and practices. Furthermore, they exercise their own *creativity*. In the process of solving technical problems in creative ways, children develop confidence in their learning potential. Clever or creative projects may be difficult to make, and the process can be frustrating. Just like in the playground, where children need to learn to play on the monkey bars without throwing tantrums, children using ScratchJr must learn how to manage their own frustration—an important step toward the development of confidence in their ability to learn new skills.

Classrooms that foster a culture in which it is expected that things may not work and might be difficult facilitate this process. As children program different projects, they gradually realize their ability to find solutions by trying multiple times, by using different strategies, or by asking for help (Bers, 2010).

The PTD framework calls for coding experiences that promote *collaboration*. This is tricky when working on a device that has only one screen. Although children can work in groups, the design of the tablet itself puts only one child in control. Children can discuss their ideas as a team, within the limitations of their developmental abilities. Young children are learning how to work together as they get out of the phase of parallel play. Having one single object to manipulate amongst a group of multiple children might pose some challenges. There is no design feature in ScratchJr specifically conceived to promote collaboration between children. The platform is a tablet designed for a single user. Thus, as seen earlier, collaboration is not about the tool, but about the teaching strategies that surround it.

The same is true for *communication*: while the playground structure fosters interaction because children need to negotiate space, a tablet directs the attention to itself. Although two children might be sitting next to each other working on ScratchJr, it is not the tool that will promote conversation, but the pedagogical choices and teaching strategies used with it. This emphasizes the importance of designing a curriculum that is aligned with the PTD framework. Otherwise, it is too easy to forget that when teaching to code in early childhood, we must also teach children how to communicate.

Along the same lines, the playground itself doesn't foster a sense of community, but the neighborhood can put in place practices to help build community around the playground. *Community building* activities, popularized in early childhood by the Reggio Emilia approach, promote each child's contribution to the wider community. In ScratchJr we added a "sharing" capability so children can share their projects with teachers and loved ones. We are also working on an online support network for adult users. Furthermore, we are organizing ScratchJr family days that bring together parents, children, siblings, and grandparents to work together on their coding projects and learn from each other.

The PTD framework reminds us of the importance of making *choices of conduct*. On the playground, children are often faced with challenges: should they cut the line for the slide or patiently wait their turn? Should they take home the nice yellow truck forgotten in the sandbox, or leave it because there is a chance that its owner will come get it later? While these dilemmas are presented every day on the playground, in a coding environment, it is harder to observe them. There are the obvious classroom situations, such as being a good partner and sharing the tablet with someone else, but there are also subtler ways.

For example, after Johnny is done with his project, should he make himself available to help others in the classroom or should he quietly do something else? Should Mary constantly ask for help when she encounters a difficult problem, or should she first try her best, as not to monopolize her teacher's attention? It is not the ScratchJr programming app that will invite children to make choices of conduct to provoke examination of values and exploration of character traits. It is, once again, the pedagogical choices of the teacher and the setup of the learning environment.

ScratchJr provides multiple ways of doing the same thing—thus, the need to choose. Just like in the playground, coding must provide opportunities for children to experiment with "what if" questions and consider potential consequences of their own choices. The moral and ethical dimensions are present in all realms of life, even when coding. When designing

132

ScratchJr we carefully kept the playground metaphor in sight. When we found ourselves limited by the tool itself, we developed curriculum and activities to help teachers and parents create playful learning environments to promote the 6 Cs of PTD. However, although we tried our best, we are limited by the on-screen format of the tablet. Much of the magic of what happens in the playground is because children are free to move around and experiment with their bodies, not only their minds.

On the playground, when children are running around and mastering all kinds of climbing structures, they are not only developing their gross motor skills—much needed in early childhood—but they are engaging in cognitive activities through their bodies. The ability to play in the space and to manipulate tangible objects might contribute to their understanding of more complex, abstract ideas. Furthermore, objects in the playground do not mediate children's interactions, face-to-face communication, or eye contact. In contrast, tablets do. Through my other project, KIBO, I was able to address some of these issues. The next chapter will expand on this.

References

Bers, M. U. (2010). The tangible K robotics program: Applied computational thinking for young children. *Early Childhood Research and Practice, 12*(2), 1–20.

Bers, M. U. (2012). *Designing digital experiences for positive youth development: From playpen to playground.* Cary, NC: Oxford.

Bers, M. U., & Resnick, M. (2015). *The official ScratchJr book.* San Francisco, CA: No Starch Press.

Flannery, L. P., Kazakoff, E. R., Bontá, P., Silverman, B., Bers, M. U., & Resnick, M. (2013). Designing ScratchJr: Support for early childhood learning through computer programming. In *Proceedings of the 12th International Conference on Interaction Design and Children (IDC '13).* ACM, New York, NY, USA (1–10). doi: 10.1145/2485760.2485785

Lakoff, G., & Johnson, M. (1980). The metaphorical structure of the human conceptual system. *Cognitive science, 4*(2), 195–208.

Lee, M.S.C. (2014). *Teaching tools, teacher's rules: ScratchJr in the classroom* (Master's Thesis). Retrieved from http://ase.tufts.edu/devtech/Theses/Melissa%20SC%20Lee%20Thesis.pdf

Papert, S. (1980). *Mindstorms: Children, computers, and powerful ideas.* New York: Basic Books.

Portelance, D. J. (2015). *Code and tell: An exploration of peer interviews and computational thinking with ScratchJr in the early childhood classroom* (Master's Thesis). Retrieved from http://ase.tufts.edu/devtech/Theses/DPortelance_2015.pdf

Portelance, D. J., & Bers, M. U. (2015). Code and tell: Assessing young children's learning of computational thinking using peer video interviews with ScratchJr. In *Proceedings of the 14th International Conference on Interaction Design and Children (IDC '15).* ACM, Boston, MA, USA.

10 | KIBO

Ezra, Mark, and Sarah are in kindergarten. During their social studies unit, they have been learning about Alaska and the Iditarod sled dog race that happens every March. They chose a musher, a strong man or woman who leads the dogs on a sled across Alaska, and followed the path on the internet, cheering for their team to win the race. They learned the names of each of the dogs, their needs and habits, and the different things that mushers must carry to survive the harsh weather.

On their classroom wall, there is a huge map of Alaska, marked with the different checkpoints across the state of Alaska, from Willow to Nome. Ezra, Mark, and Sarah learned geography by studying the race and its different routes. They also learned the Iditarod's history through a book that Mrs. Dolan read aloud to them. In 1925, a diphtheria epidemic threatened Nome, and Nome's supply of antitoxin had expired. The nearest antitoxin was found in Anchorage, about 500 miles away, near Willow. The only way to get the antitoxin to Nome was by sled dog. A safe route was organized and the 20-pound cylinder of serum was sent, first by train and then by 20 mushers and more than 100 dogs. The dogs ran in relays. Since then, every year the Iditarod sled dog race re-enacts this event, and the children in Mrs. Dolan's kindergarten class learn about it.

Ezra, Mark, and Sarah studied Alaska's towns and geography. They learned about the hard terrains and the easy paths. They have been doing research on the subject for over two weeks. But today is their time to put all their knowledge to the test; not by passing an exam or completing a worksheet, but by re-creating the Iditarod race with KIBO robots.

Mrs. Dolan gave them the challenge to build and program their robots to travel from one checkpoint to another, starting in Willow and ending in Nome, carrying all the things mushers must carry, as well as the pretend serum for the sick children. Each team receives a piece of thick cardboard with two checkpoints marked at the ends and a KIBO robot. They first need to draw the route from checkpoint to checkpoint and decorate the cardboard to resemble the geography of that region. Second, they need to build their robots with a platform that can carry everything needed, including a safe way to transport the serum until reaching the next checkpoint and passing it on to the next team. They need to do sturdy engineering because the Alaskan terrain is bumpy, and they do not want everything to fall off the robotic sled. Finally, they need to program their robots to travel safely from checkpoint to checkpoint.

Mrs. Dolan put together the cardboards on the floor in the library making a huge floor map of Alaska. They needed a big space to work in; they chose the library because the classroom wasn't big enough. Mrs. Dolan assigned "jobs" to the children within each of the groups: the artist, the engineer, and the programmer. She asked them to come forward to the tables that had the needed materials. Some children complained because they did not like their assigned jobs. Mrs. Dolan assured them that all children would experience every job and spend the same amount of time at each task.

Mark walks to the art materials table and grabs markers and crayons as well as recyclable materials, cotton balls, and glue. He wants to decorate the cardboard with snow, trees, mountains, and a family of foxes. Both Sarah and Ezra want to be the engineers. After some back and forth, they agree that Sarah will take on that role first and Ezra will be second. Sarah walks to the robot table and grabs three motors, three wheels, and two wooden platforms. She also picks up a KIBO light bulb and a bunch of sensors. She is still not sure what those are, but she wants to have them. Ezra, the programmer, walks to a table full of bins with different wooden blocks labeled with colors, images, and words he cannot read, with a peg on one side and a hole on the other. That is KIBO's programming language. Following Mrs. Dolan's instructions, Ezra chooses a green begin block, to start the program, and a red end block, to end the program. And then he grabs as many other colorful blocks as he can carry in his hands.

Shortly, the three children meet again at their spot on the Alaska floor map. The library becomes noisy as each group starts their work. There is a lot to decide. Sarah builds a robot with two motors and wheels at the sides and a motor and a moving platform on top. She adds the light bulb and a few sensors: an ear to detect sound, a telescope to detect distance, and an eye to detect light. The robot is ready to go, but it must be programmed, otherwise it will not move. Mark wants the robot to follow the path he drew on the cardboard. Ezra is not sure how many blue "forward" blocks are needed in between the green start and the red end blocks. He puts together a sequence of four forward blocks and tells Sarah to try it out. Sarah starts scanning the blocks. She holds the robot and makes sure it is awake by looking at the red light coming out of its scanner. She aligns the scanner light with the barcodes on the blocks and starts scanning the blocks one by one. Mark helps her by saying "yes" every time a green light on the robot turns on, signaling a successful scan. When they are done programming KIBO, they place it on the cardboard trails to see what happens.

"It is not running long enough," says Sarah. "It needs to have at least two more forward blocks." "I don't think so," replies Ezra, "I think we need five more forward blocks." A few exchanges follow, in which children are busy estimating distance and predicting how many more steps are needed, and then they decide to try things out. After some trial and error, they make it work. Now they are ready to make the journey a little bit more fancy. They decide that the robot will start to move once it hears a clap, marking the fact that the serum is on board. They also decide that before arriving at the last checkpoint it will shake and turn its red light on to alert the next team to get ready.

As children start programming their KIBO sleds and practicing the relay race, the classroom becomes a playground. Different children are busy at different tasks. Some are drawing and decorating, others are programming with wooden blocks, some are using tape and plastic cups to make sturdy structures for the serum, some are experimenting with different sensors, some are doing math to calculate distances, a few are running from checkpoint to checkpoint cheering on their robots. All of them are very engaged.

We can hear laughs and sighs of frustration, as well as lots of questions and answers. Children are interacting amongst themselves and with the adults in the room. They are fully immersed and focused in the activity. Mrs. Dolan has planned a trial run before the end of the period, because family and friends are invited to come on Friday morning, at drop off, to see the robotic race and cheer for the different teams. Most parents can't wait to see how their young kindergartners, who mostly do not know how to read and write, can program robots.

KIBO: The Tool

KIBO is a robot kit specifically designed for children ages 4–7 years old. Young children learn by doing, thus KIBO provides opportunities for doing different things. Children can build their own robot, program it to do what they want, and decorate it with art supplies. KIBO gives children the chance to make their ideas physical and tangible—without requiring screen time from PCs, tablets, or smartphones.

The concept, prototypes, and research for KIBO were born in my DevTech research group in 2011 through generous funding from the National Science Foundation (NSF DRL 0735657). KIBO became commercially available worldwide in 2014 through KinderLab Robotics, a company I co-founded with Mitch Rosenberg (see www.kinderlabrobotics.com).

Designed with a playground approach, KIBO supports children in making almost anything: a character from a story, a carousel, a dancer, a dog sled. The possibilities are endless, as wide as children's own imaginations. The child puts together a sequence of instructions (a program) using the wooden KIBO blocks. Then, they scan the blocks with the KIBO body to tell the robot what to do. Finally, they press a button and the robot comes "alive." KIBO engages children in becoming programmers, engineers, problem solvers, designers, artists, dancers, choreographers, and writers.

As a robotics construction kit, KIBO has hardware (the robot body, wheels, motors, a light output, a variety of sensors, and art platforms) (see Figure 10.1) and software (a tangible programming language composed of interlocking wooden blocks).

Each wooden block has a colorful label with an icon, text, and a bar code, as well as a hole on an end and a peg on the other (see Figure 10.2). These wooden blocks contain no electronic or digital components. Instead, the KIBO robot has an embedded scanner. The scanner allows users to scan the barcodes on the wooden blocks and send a program to their robot instantaneously. No computer, tablet, or other form of "screen-time" is required to program with KIBO. This design choice is aligned with the American Academy of Pediatrics' recommendation that young children should have a limited amount of screen time per day (American Academy of Pediatrics, 2016). KIBO's programming language contains over 18 different individual programming wooden blocks. Some of those blocks are simple, while others represent complex programming concepts including repeat loops, conditionals, and nesting statements.

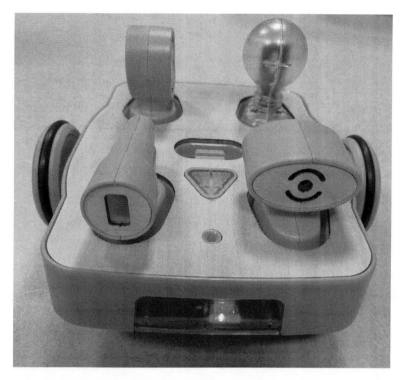

Figure 10.1 KIBO robot with sensors and light output attached.

Figure 10.2 Sample KIBO program. This program tells the robot to spin, turn a blue light on, and shake.

The use of wooden blocks for KIBO was inspired by early ideas from tangible programming. In the mid-1970s, Radia Perlman, a researcher at the MIT Logo Lab (Perlman, 1976), first introduced the idea of tangible programming, which was then revived nearly two decades later (Suzuki & Kato, 1995). Since then, several tangible languages have been created in several different research labs around the world (e.g., McNerney, 2004; Wyeth &

Purchase, 2002; Smith, 2007; Horn & Jacob, 2007; Horn, Crouser, & Bers, 2012; Google Research, 2016).

A tangible programming language, like any other type of computer language, is a tool for telling a processor what to do. With a text-based language, a programmer uses words such as BEGIN, IF, and REPEAT to instruct a computer. With a visual language, such as ScratchJr, words are replaced by pictures, and programs are expressed by arranging and connecting icons on the screen. Tangible languages, instead, use physical objects to represent the various aspects of computer programming (Manches & Price, 2011).

With KIBO, children arrange and connect wooden blocks to give commands to their robots. The physical properties of these objects are exploited to express and enforce syntax. For example, the KIBO begin block doesn't have a hole, only a peg, because there is nothing that can be placed before the begin; and the end block doesn't have a peg, because there is no instruction that can go after the program ends (see Figure 10.3). The language syntax in KIBO (i.e., a sequential connection of blocks) is designed to support and reinforce sequencing skills in young children.

Why a programming language made of wooden blocks? Wooden blocks are naturally familiar and comfortable for young children and teachers and can be found in almost every kindergarten classroom. They belong to a tradition of learning manipulatives already used in early childhood classrooms to teach shapes, size, and colors (Froebel, 1826; Montessori & Gutek, 2004). Table 10.1 presents a list of currently available programming

Figure 10.3 KIBO's begin and end blocks.

Table 10.1 KIBO's block language

KIBO Block	Block Function
BEGIN	This is the first block in every program, tells robot to start
END	This is the last block in every program, tells robot to stop
FORWARD	Makes KIBO move forward several inches
BACKWARD	Makes KIBO move backward several inches
SPIN	Makes KIBO turn around in a circle
SHAKE	Makes KIBO shake from left to right
TURN LEFT	Makes KIBO turn to face the left
TURN RIGHT	Makes KIBO turn to face the right
WHITE LIGHT ON	Turns on KIBO's light bulb with a white light
RED LIGHT ON	Turns on KIBO's light bulb with a red light

(Continued)

Table 10.1 (Continued)

KIBO Block	Block Function
BLUE LIGHT ON	Turns on KIBO's light bulb with a blue light
SING	Makes KIBO "sing" (i.e., play a series of automated tunes)
BEEP	Makes KIBO beep once
PLAY △ PLAY ○ PLAY □	Plays back a sound recorded with KIBO's sound recorder
WAIT FOR CLAP	When the sound sensor is attached, this block makes KIBO stop and wait for a sound before continuing to the next action in the program
REPEAT	This block is used to open a "repeat loop" (like opening a set of parentheses). A repeat loops allows users to separate out a series of blocks for KIBO to repeat a particular number of times.
END REPEAT	This block is used to close a "repeat loop" (like closing a set of parentheses)
IF	This block is used to open a "conditional statement" (like opening a set of parentheses). A conditional statement allows KIBO to decide what to do based on sensor input.
END IF	This block is used to close a "conditional statement" (like closing a set of parentheses)
(parameter blocks)	In addition to the 18 blocks in KIBO's current language, there are 12 parameters that can be used to modify the repeat loops and conditional statements to tell KIBO how many times to repeat actions or what type of sensor input to react to.

blocks for KIBO. As new sensor modules are being developed, new programming blocks are also released.

In addition to the tangible programming language, the KIBO robot comes with sensors and actuators (motors and light bulb), as well as art platforms. These modules can be interchangeably combined on the robot body.

Each sensor's aesthetic is designed to convey meaning (i.e., the ear-shaped part is a sound sensor; the eye-shaped part is a light sensor; and the telescope-shaped part is a distance sensor). During the late pre-operational stage of cognitive development (ages 4–6), children extend and apply culturally learned symbol systems to interactions with the physical and social world—thus, our explicit emphasis on design features with symbolic representations.

Sensing is the ability of the robot to collect and respond to information on its environment. The sound sensor is used to differentiate the two concepts of "loud" and "quiet." Using the sound sensor, the robot can be programmed to do something when it is loud, and do something else when it gets quiet, or vice versa. The light sensor is used to differentiate the two concepts of "dark" and "light." The robot can be programmed to do something when it is light out, and do something else when it gets dark, or vice versa. Finally, the distance sensor is used to detect whether the robot is getting nearer to something or further from it. The robot can be programmed to do something when it gets near something, and do something else when it moves away from it. A sound recorder module includes both input and output properties (see Figure 10.5). This sound recorder allows KIBO to record sound (input), and it can also be programmed with a corresponding block to play back the sound (output). The light output is shaped like a lightbulb and is made of a different color plastic (transparent) than the sensors, so children do not get confused between the concepts of inputs and outputs (see Figure 10.4).

The use of sensors is well aligned with most early childhood curriculum that engages children in exploring both human and animal sensors. For example, in most early childhood classrooms young children are already exploring their own five senses (sight, sound, taste, touch, and smell) and they can apply this knowledge to an exploration of KIBO's robotic sensors. They can liken their own sense of sound, for example, to KIBO's sound sensor.

Three motors are included with the robot, two can be connected to the opposite sides of the robot, for mobility, and one motor can be located on

Figure 10.4 Three sensors (from left: distance, sound, and light) and light-bulb.

Figure 10.5 KIBO's sound recorder and corresponding blocks.

top, for rotation of an attached element such as the art platform. Children can decide which motors they want to connect, but they cannot control the speed of the motors. This design feature highlights the importance of creating flexible and stimulating learning environments, and at the same time prevents the overload of young children's working memory and limited attention span.

Figure 10.6 Art supplies and KIBO's art platforms and whiteboard.

The KIBO kit also contains art platforms and expression modules for artistic exploration (see Figure 10.6). These can be used for children to personalize their projects with crafts materials and foster STEAM integration. The art platforms are attached to the top of KIBO and can be static or mobile, and provide a place for children to creatively use different materials. Additionally, the motorized art stage allows for more versatility in robotic design. For example, children can construct kinetic sculptures and animated dioramas. The expression module includes a whiteboard, markers, and flagpole. Children can decorate the whiteboard with pictures and words or they create their own flag out of paper or fabric to insert into the flagpole.

KIBO: The Process

In the beginning, back in 2011, KIBO had a different name. We called it KIWI (Kids Invent with Imagination). Students in my DevTech research group chose that acronym. However, later, we discovered potential conflicts with that name, so we switched it to KIBO. We liked the sound of it. We also thought it was a way to remind children of the words kids and bot (from robot).

KIBO went through many prototypes before it made it out into the world. The National Science Foundation funded research on each of the iterations (DRL-1118897, DRL-0735657), and we received additional money from a successful Kickstarter campaign. At every stage of development and testing we collaborated with early educators, children, and specialists to create an age-appropriate robotic kit that would be intuitive and engaging, but also challenging.

We wanted KIBO to support developmentally appropriate practices, often shortened to DAP, in early childhood (Bredekamp, 1987). DAP is a teaching approach grounded in research on how young children develop and learn and in what is known about effective early education (Bredekamp, 1987; Copple & Bredekamp, 2009). We also wanted it to become a playground for tangible coding in which children could encounter powerful ideas from computer science and develop computational thinking, while engaging with the six positive behaviors of the PTD framework. Based on this, KIBO was designed to be:

- Age appropriate: its design features establish reasonable expectations of what is interesting, safe, achievable, and challenging for young children;

- Individually appropriate: it can be used by children with different learning styles, background knowledge, exposure, and skills in the technological domain, and different developmental abilities and self-regulatory skills;

- Socially and culturally appropriate: the use of KIBO can be integrated with multiple disciplines and can support the teaching of interdisciplinary curriculum that meets state and nationally mandated frameworks.

Our early research with KIBO was informed by doing pilot studies where we used commercially available robotics kits such as LEGO WeDo and LEGO MINDSTORMS, both designed for older children. We learned from observing children's challenges and discoveries and from talking with teachers about their experiences. Most of that early research is summarized in my book *Blocks to Robots* (Bers, 2008). For some of the studies, we used the commercially available software that came with those kits; for others, my then student Mike Horn connected the LEGO MINDSTORMS yellow brick to a tangible programming language he developed as part of his doctoral work called TERN (Horn, Crouser, & Bers, 2012). Later on, two other students in my group, Jordan Crouser and David Kiger, extended this project and created the language CHERP (Creative Hybrid Environment for Robotic Programming) (Bers, 2010). Both TERN and CHERP required a standard webcam connected to a desktop or laptop computer to take a picture of the program, which included blocks or puzzle pieces with circular bar-code-like easily readable by a vision software. The computer then converted the picture into digital code. We conducted lots of research to understand what worked and what didn't with those robot kits, and what needed to change (Sullivan, Elkin, & Bers, 2015).

From pilot testing and focus groups we learned that KIBO needed parts that could be physically and intuitively easy to connect, and it would be best if it was programmed without a computer. We also heard that children and teachers wanted to attach a variety of crafts and recycled materials to the core robotic parts to make different types of creations, both stationary and mobile. Based on these general principles, we developed a list that identified desired design features and, through NSF funding, hired a consultant team to develop an initial prototype that instantiated these ideas. The first KIBO prototype (then called "KIWI") was programmed with CHERP and required the use of a computer and a webcam to take pictures of the blocks and send the program to the robot through a USB cable. This robot was constructed out of solid wood and opaque blue plastic for the modules (see Figure 10.7).

We hand built ten first prototypes and tested them in focus groups, professional development workshops, and the classroom (Bers, Seddighin, & Sullivan, 2013; Sullivan, Elkin, & Bers, 2015; Sullivan & Bers, 2015). We asked teachers both about our design choices for KIBO, as well as its suitability for: 1) teaching foundational engineering concepts of sturdy building and construction; 2) teaching foundational coding concepts such as sequencing, repeat loops, and conditional branching; and 3) open-ended creativity and artistic design.

Teachers were generally excited and were drawn to the use of wood and the simplicity of our first design. However, they also pointed out several impediments for using this original design in a sustained and feasible way in the classroom. Teachers indicated that programming the robot should use minimal or no computer equipment. Teachers felt this was important

Figure 10.7 KIWI prototype.

from both a logistical standpoint (e.g., most teachers did not have enough computers in a kindergarten classroom and had limited access to those resources) and from a developmentally appropriate standpoint (e.g., teachers worried about screen time and about children manipulating a keyboard and mouse).

Data were collected from 32 early childhood educators in 2013 on their attitudes, opinions, and experiences to inform the re-design of the prototype (Bers, Seddighin, & Sullivan, 2013). Results show that this first version of KIBO was successful in engaging children in foundational programming skills. However, its robotic parts were too easy to assemble and did not sufficiently engage children in engineering problem-solving or creative artistic design.

From early testing with that first prototype, we learned a lot and hired a new team of consultants, as well as engaged many volunteers, teachers, and students to work with us on the next prototype. This second prototype had a 3D printed KIBO body, as opposed to wood. It also included an embedded scanner, eliminating the need to use a computer. This directly addressed the teachers' concerns about availability of computers in early childhood classrooms and screen time for young children. Additionally, instead of having a "magical black box" with the electronic components inside the robot's body, the newer KIBO prototype had a clear plastic bottom, allowing children to see the wires, batteries, microprocessor, and other parts involved in making the robot function (see Figure 10.8).

Furthermore, in order to address the need of more "engineering," we designed the wheels to connect to the motors in two different ways, prompting children to test how changing the wheels' orientation makes the

Figure 10.8 Transparent underside of KIBO robot.

robot move differently. The shapes and looks of both sensors and light output components were also redesigned to address earlier pilot testing with children. For example, we changed the distance sensor, which was originally a blue unrecognizable shape as a telescope, to look like a telescope. In addition, we included the use of art platforms to provide more ways for children to build and create, extending the use of KIBO to incorporate arts, crafts, and recycled materials along with the robotic components.

The Complexity of Simplicity

As the new prototype was built, the circuit board, robotic components, and robot body changed in their looks and functionality. However, the new prototype kept its core design principle: simplicity. KIBO has a "plug and play" connection system. The robot parts or modules can connect and disconnect intuitively and easily. They are functional with no further steps other than plugging them in. Additionally, KIBO's design forces the correct orientation of parts.

Each basic programming instruction corresponds to one robotic action. Each robotic component corresponds to one function. For example, only one module is needed for each action (i.e., the motor module is needed to move the robot gears, connectors, etc.). This design choice supports correspondence, a cognitive developmental milestone for young children that is a foundational skill for later academic success.

There are a limited number of ways to construct and program KIBO. The robot has a limited number of component types and limited number of possible combinations for these components. There are limited control points for the child (e.g., children can tell the robot to go forward or backward, but not how fast). Sensors sense presence or absence of stimuli, but not the degree of variation within the stimuli. This design principle was guided by studies that show that children of this age typically have limited working memory capacity, and are just beginning to hold multi-step instructions in their heads (Shonkoff, Duncan, Fisher, Magnuson, & Raver, 2011).

The aesthetic features of KIBO have remained purposefully plain throughout each prototype iteration. The "unfinished" look invites children to complete the robot using their own imaginative creations. Much like a blank canvas or un-sculpted clay, KIBO inspires children to add to it. This supports a variety of sensory and aesthetic experiences.

The robot is designed to be easily manipulated by a young child without falling apart. Pieces are large enough to be assembled safely by young children (i.e., there's nothing they can swallow). KIBO remains intact while being handled and used in ways typical of 4-year-olds (e.g., dropping, running into walls, etc.). This supports children developing fine motor skills and extending their self-regulation practices.

The design of KIBO is aimed at shifting the problem-solving focus away from low-level problems (i.e., syntax and connection errors) towards high-level problem solving (i.e., creating a program that matches a goal). The robot body has the right weight and size to be manipulated by a young child's hands. The size of the robot allows it to be shareable to promote social interaction. This allows children to engage in problem solving in a developmentally appropriate way that takes into consideration their ability for self-regulation. Furthermore, it promotes a journey towards computational literacy that enables the use of the robot for personal expression and communication.

KIBO can be easily integrated with literacy. The programming language pairs iconic images and simple words and allows children to explore sequencing, a foundational skill for literacy development. Developmentally appropriate practice calls for interdisciplinary curriculum. KIBO supports integrated learning. For example, children encounter concepts such as number, size, measurement, distance, time, counting, directionality, and estimation. At the same time, they are learning and applying new vocabulary words, communicating with teachers and peers, and writing and drawing notes in their design journals.

From the Lab to the World

Over the years my DevTech research group conducted many studies with the 3D printed KIBO prototypes. This research showed that beginning in pre-kindergarten, children could master basic robotics and programming skills, while the older children (first and second grade) could master increasingly complex concepts in the same amount of time (Sullivan & Bers, 2015). We iteratively re-designed the prototypes based on pilot studies with children and teachers (Sullivan, Elkin, & Bers, 2015).

Alongside KIBO we developed curriculum, teaching materials, and assessments tools. These materials include games, songs, and activities (many of which can be done without the use of the robot or blocks) that reinforce the computational and engineering concepts introduced by KIBO. We have developed nearly a dozen curriculum units that integrate KIBO with STEM disciplines as well as social sciences, literacy, and the arts. These curriculum units are aligned with national and international STEM standards. Some examples are: *How Things Move* (explores foundational physics connections related to motion, light, and friction, while engaging children in engineering and computational thinking); *Sensing the World Around Us* (looks at how sensors work, particularly the three KIBO sensors: Light, Distance, and Sound); *Dances from Around the World* (engages children in making and programming robots that perform dances from around the world); *Patterns All Around Us* (integrates a study of math and patterns with robotics). At the same time, we created an online resource for educators, the Early Childhood Robotics Network, to access these free curriculum resources. This can be found at www.tkroboticsnetwork.ning.com.

As time went on, the word about our KIBO prototype started to spread. When giving talks, I was often asked by parents and teachers, researchers and practitioners: "How can I get a KIBO robot kit?" For some time, I did not have a good answer, because KIBOs were only hand-built prototypes in our DevTech lab. I grew frustrated and often found myself wondering what the point of my research was if we couldn't make it available to others.

During conversations with NSF, I learned about the Small Business Innovation Research (SBIR) program that could help me take my research on KIBO out of the lab into a commercial enterprise. I knew I had to partner with someone with a different set of skills, as I did not know much about what makes a business viable. During a walk in Walden Pond, near Boston, my friend Mitch Rosenberg, veteran executive at several robotics start-ups, decided to join me to pursue a long-time dream of his: improving STEM education.

Together we co-founded KinderLab Robotics, Inc., with the goal of commercializing KIBO and making it available worldwide. KinderLab Robotics received initial funding from the National Science Foundation through an SBIR Phase I, Phase IB, and Phase II grants. In addition, a successful Kickstarter campaign allowed us to supplement those funds and KIBO was first made commercially available through KinderLab Robotics in 2014.

KIBO Today

Since its launch in 2014, KIBO has made it into private and public schools, museums and libraries, after school programs, and summer camps, both in the U.S. and abroad. KIBO has been used to teach a variety of curricular topics ranging from science to literacy and even social-emotional concepts, and pilot studies have been done with children on the autism spectrum.

At a local public school in Somerville, MA, early childhood teachers implemented a robotics curriculum in grades K–2 with the goal of fostering prosocial behaviors and community building. Students also programmed their robots to demonstrate respectful behaviors and school rules that kids often forget. For example, one student created a robot that reminded students to listen to their teacher during circle time. Another student created a robot to demonstrate walking through the hallway quietly and making lots of noise only when it reached the playground.

In a summer camp, KIBO was used to bring literacy and the arts to life in a playful way. In this one-week camp, students read a different book each day and programmed their robots to "act out" their favorite scenes from each book as well as alternative endings. As a final project, children read the iconic children's book *Where the Wild Things Are* by Maurice Sendak. Children designed and built their own KIBO monsters inspired by the story and programmed them to act out the "Wild Rumpus" scene (i.e., a wild monster party).

In another KIBO class, students explored robotics and programming with the theme of "Superheroes." They began with a group discussion answering the question, "What makes someone a hero?" Initially, children focused on super-abilities such as flying, super strength, and invisibility. These are the characteristics that their favorite cartoon superheroes like Superman and the Incredibles have. However, when prompted to think of super villains or classic "bad guys" who also had many of these super abilities, the children came to a new conclusion: superheroes strive to "do good" in the world. This class came up with a long list of what they called "everyday heroes" that included firefighters, teachers, doctors, and even their parents and friends. They also discussed all the ways they can be "school superheroes" by helping their teachers, playing with someone at recess who is alone, and respecting one another. They created KIBO Superhero Bots inspired by the real everyday heroes they learned about, as well as their favorite fantasy-inspired superhero abilities. For example, many children used sensors to give their Super KIBO "super senses" that allow it to perform extraordinary tasks. One boy used the KIBO's sound sensor to tell a story about how his robot hero listens for people calling for help and then goes to help them.

KIBO provides a playground for coding. As evidenced by the diversity of projects described earlier, children can playfully program their own projects, while engaging in the six positive behaviors (6 Cs), proposed by the PTD framework and reviewed in Chapter 8, to promote playground coding experiences for young children: content creation, creativity, collaboration, communication, choices of conduct, and community building (Bers, 2012).

KIBO and Positive Technological Development

KIBO involves children in making their own robots and programming their behaviors (i.e., creating content). The engineering design process required for building and the computational thinking involved in programming foster *competence* in computer literacy and technological fluency.

The classroom practice of keeping design journals during the creation process makes transparent to the children (as well as teachers and parents) their own thinking, their own learning trajectories, and the project's evolution over time. Like the scientific method, the formal steps of the engineering design process—posing a problem, doing research, planning, developing a prototype, testing, redesigning, and sharing solutions—gives students a tool for systematically addressing a problem (see Figure 10.9).

KIBO promotes creativity, as opposed to efficiency, in problem solving; the approach is informed by the original meaning of the word *engineering*, which derives from the Latin *ingenium*, meaning, "innate quality, mental power, clever invention." Through the process of solving technical problems in creative ways, children develop confidence in their learning potential.

Most educational robotic programs for older children, such as the National Robotics Challenge and FIRST (For Inspiration and Recognition of Science and Technology), are set up as competitions in which robots have to accomplish a given task, usually with the goal of outperforming other robots. However, research has shown that females tend to not respond well

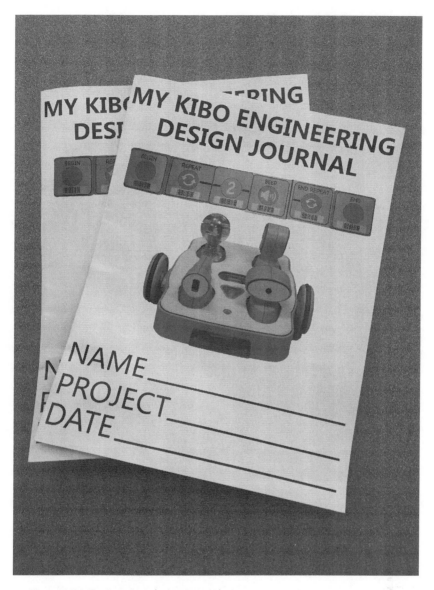

Figure 10.9 Engineering design journals.

to teaching strategies that stress competition; such strategies also might not always be appropriate in the early childhood setting (Bers, 2008). With KIBO, and as shown in Mrs. Dolan's class, the learning environment, instead of focusing on competition, promotes sharing and caring about each other.

The PTD framework speaks to the importance of providing opportunities for communication. While most of the work with KIBOs happens on teams, we also encourage structured ways for young children to communicate not only on a one-on-one basis with peers and teachers but also to the whole group. During technology circles, the teacher invites children to show their projects and asks questions such as, "What worked as expected and what didn't?", "What are you trying to accomplish?", "What do you need to know in order to make it happen?" The teacher then uses children's projects and questions to highlight powerful ideas.

Learning with KIBO is "hard fun" and a lot of work. Following the PTD framework, there is always an open house to invite friends and family to see and play with the KIBO projects. Similar to what happened in Mrs. Dolan's kindergarten class, most adults can't believe the sophisticated projects young children can create until they get to see them. The public displays make learning visible to others, but also to the children themselves.

The last C proposed by the PTD framework, choices of conduct, reminds teachers of providing opportunities for children to experiment with "what if" questions and potential consequences. However, choices of conduct are not only made by children; teachers also make them. For example, if the KIBO sensors are sorted by types and placed in bins in the center of the room (instead of given to each child or group as a presorted robotic kit), children learn to take what they need without depleting the bins of the "most wanted" pieces. They also learn how to negotiate. The PTD approach guides us in helping young children develop an inner compass to guide their actions in a just and responsible way, and not only to become experts at KIBO robotics.

The Singapore Case

Most of the examples above show how individual classrooms or schools, museums or libraries, are using KIBO robots in different ways. However, Singapore is implementing a nationwide project to bring KIBO, amongst other technologies, into all early childhood classrooms. Singapore, along with many other nations, is well aware of the growing need for engineering and computer education in schools. With sharp insight, Steve Leonard, the executive deputy chairman of Singapore's Infocomm Development Authority (IDA)[1] said, "As Singapore becomes a Smart Nation, our children will need to be comfortable creating with technology" (IDA Singapore, 2015). Thus, Singapore's government recently launched the "PlayMaker Programme" initiative to introduce younger children to technology (Digital News Asia, 2015). The goal of this program is to provide young children (ages 4–7) with digital tools to have fun, practice problem solving, and build confidence and creativity in a developmentally appropriate way (Digital News Asia, 2015).

According to the director of education at Singapore's Infocomm Media Development Authority (IMDA[2]), Singapore is trying to change the idea of what technology in preschool settings looks like, from a screen-based approach to a maker-centered approach (Chambers, 2015). This vision is consistent with my playground approach, and therefore I was invited to train a first cohort of early childhood teachers as part of the PlayMaker Programme and to conduct a research study following different centers to understand learning outcomes with KIBO. One hundred sixty preschool centers across Singapore were given a suite of age and developmentally appropriate technological toys that engage children with robotics, programming, building, and engineering, including: Bee-Bot, Circuit Stickers, littleBits, and KIBO robotics. In addition, early childhood educators also received training and on-ground support on how to use and teach with each of these tools embedded into the center's curriculum.

Our study focused on research questions such as:

1. What programming concepts do preschool children master after being introduced to KIBO?

2. How engaged were children with the different aspects of the PTD framework while participating in the KIBO robotics curriculum?

3. What was this experience like for the participating teachers? What areas of this initiative did they feel were successful, and what areas need improvement?

Our exploration of the KIBO robot was situated within our DevTech curricular unit called *Dances from Around the World*. The *Dances from Around the World* unit is designed to engage children with STEAM content through an integration of music, dance, and culture using engineering and programming tools (DevTech, 2015). This unit was chosen specifically to appeal to the multicultural nature of the Singaporean community. Singapore has a bilingual education policy where all students in government schools are taught English as their primary language. In addition to English, students also learn another language called their "Mother Tongue," which might be Mandarin, Malay, or Tamil. Because the students in Singapore speak different languages and have different cultural backgrounds, the *Dances from Around the World* curriculum easily integrated into cultural appreciation and awareness units already typically taught in the preschool classes. The implementation of the *Dances from Around the World* curriculum was rooted in PTD framework.

Over the course of approximately seven weeks, teachers introduced their students to new robotics or programming concepts. While most teachers were generally novices when it came to teaching with technology, this did not present an obstacle for their teaching. "Even though we don't know, we're still very interested in it. We just touch it and learn and see how it works," summarized a young teacher (Sullivan & Bers, 2017). Lessons took place for approximately one hour once a week, leading up to a final project. Concepts from basic sequencing through conditional statements were covered. For the final project, students worked in pairs or small groups to design, build, and program a cultural dance from around the world. This activity drew on the accumulation of students' knowledge throughout the curriculum. By the culmination of the final project, all groups had a functional KIBO robotics project that they demonstrated during the final presentations.

All groups used at least two motors and were successful at integrating arts, crafts, and recycled materials to represent the dance of their choosing. Many groups also used sensors and advanced programming concepts such as repeat loops and conditional statements (Sullivan & Bers, 2017). Students and teachers were also successful at integrating the arts in other ways through music, dance, costumes, and performances. For example, some groups decorated their KIBOs to represent different ethnicities in Singapore and chose music from that ethnicity. Other groups had children dressed up in clothing to represent the same cultures their robots were representing. They performed, danced, and sang along with the robots. Their classrooms became playgrounds. What facilitated this? The design of KIBO as a developmentally appropriate tool and the open-ended nature of the curriculum, as well as the good alignment between the PTD framework and the pedagogical approach of these Singapore educational settings.

Adeline Yeo, senior manager of Education/Sector Innovation for Singapore's Infocomm Media Development Authority (IMDA), after visiting a Learning Festival organized by one of the operators who has implemented PlayMaker and KIBO in 33 preschool centers, shares how impressed she was to see the children and teachers's effort. She recounts one particular experience: "The teachers tried different programs to have KIBO go round and round like a carousel. In the end, they removed the wheels and programmed it to turn left forever. Great problem solving and collaboration involved. We are turning teachers into engineers!" (see Figure 10.10).

Figure 10.10 KIBO Carousel created by teachers at a Learning Festival in Singapore.

Notes

1. Steve Leonard was the executive deputy chairman of IDA Singapore from June 2013 to June 2016.
2. IMDA was restructured from IDA in September 2016.

References

American Academy of Pediatrics Council on Communications and Media. (2016). Media and young minds. *Pediatrics, 138*(5).

Bers, M. (2008). *Blocks to robots: Learning with technology in the early childhood classroom.* New York, NY: Teachers College Press.

Bers, M. U. (2010). The tangible K robotics program: Applied computational thinking for young children. *Early Childhood Research and Practice, 12*(2).

Bers, M. U. (2012). *Designing digital experiences for positive youth development: From playpen to playground.* Cary, NC: Oxford.

Bers, M. U., Seddighin, S., & Sullivan, A. (2013). Ready for robotics: Bringing together the T and E of STEM in early childhood teacher education. *Journal of Technology and Teacher Education, 21*(3), 355–377.

Bredekamp, S. (1987). *Developmentally appropriate practice in early childhood programs serving children from birth through age 8.* National Association for the Education of Young Children.

Chambers, J. (2015). Inside Singapore's plans for robots in pre-schools. *GovInsider.*

Copple, C., & Bredekamp, S. (2009). *Developmentally appropriate practice in early childhood programs serving children from birth through age 8.* 1313 L Street NW Suite 500, Washington, DC 22205–4101: National Association for the Education of Young Children.

DevTech Research Group. (2015). *Dances from around the world robotics curriculum.* Retrieved from http://tkroboticsnetwork.ning.com/page/robotics-curriculum

Digital News Asia. (2015). IDA launches $1.5m pilot to roll out tech toys for preschoolers. Retrieved from: https://www.digitalnewsasia.com/digital-economy/ida-launches-pilot-to-roll-out-tech-toys-for-preschoolers

Froebel, F. (1826). *On the education of man (Die Menschenerziehung)*. Keilhau/Leipzig: Wienbrach.

Google, Research. (2016, June). *Project Bloks: Designing a development platform for tangible programming for children* [Position paper]. Retrieved from https://projectbloks.withgoogle.com/static/Project_Bloks_position_paper_June_2016.pdf

Horn, M. S., Crouser, R. J., & Bers, M. U. (2012). Tangible interaction and learning: The case for a hybrid approach. *Personal and Ubiquitous Computing, 16*(4), 379–389.

Horn, M. S., & Jacob, R. J. (2007). Tangible programming in the classroom with tern. In *CHI'07 extended abstracts on human factors in computing systems* (pp. 1965–1970). ACM.

IDA Singapore. (2015). *IDA supports preschool centres with technology-enabled toys to build creativity and confidence in learning*. Retrieved from www.ida.gov.sg/About-Us/Newsroom/Media-Releases/2015/IDA-supports-preschool-centres-with-technology-enabled-toys-to-build-creativity-and-confidence-in-learning

Manches, A., & Price, S. (2011). Designing learning representations around physical manipulation: Hands and objects. In *Proceedings of the 10th International Conference on Interaction Design and Children* (pp. 81–89). ACM.

McNerney, T. S. (2004). From turtles to tangible programming bricks: Explorations in physical language design. *Personal and Ubiquitous Computing, 8*(5), 326–337.

Montessori, M., & Gutek, G. L. (2004). *The Montessori method: The origins of an educational innovation: Including an abridged and annotated edition of Maria Montessori's the Montessori method*. Lanham, MD: Rowman & Littlefield Publishers.

Perlman, R. (1976). *Using Computer Technology to Provide a Creative Learning Environment for Preschool Children*. MIT Logo Memo #24, Cambridge, MA.

Shonkoff, J. P., Duncan, G. J., Fisher, P. A., Magnuson, K., & Raver, C. (2011). Building the brain's "air traffic control" system: How early experiences shape the development of executive function. Working Paper No. 11.

Smith, A. C. (2007). Using magnets in physical blocks that behave as programming objects. In *Proceedings of the 1st International Conference on Tangible and Embedded Interaction* (pp. 147–150). ACM.

Sullivan, A., & Bers, M. U. (2015). Robotics in the early childhood classroom: Learning outcomes from an 8-week robotics curriculum in pre-kindergarten through second grade. *International Journal of Technology and Design Education.* Online First.

Sullivan, A., & Bers, M. U. (2017). Dancing robots: Integrating art, music, and robotics in Singapore's early childhood centers. *International Journal of Technology and Design Education.* Online First. doi:10.1007/s10798-017-9397-0

Sullivan, A., Elkin, M., & Bers, M. U. (2015). KIBO robot demo: Engaging young children in programming and engineering. In *Proceedings of the 14th International Conference on Interaction Design and Children (IDC '15).* ACM, Boston, MA, USA.

Suzuki, H., & Kato, H. (1995). Interaction-level support for collaborative learning: Algoblock- an open programming language. In J. L Schnase & E. L. Cunnius (Eds.), *Proceedings on CSCL '95: The first international conference on computer support for collaborative learning* (pp. 349–355). Mahwah, NJ: Erlbaum.

Wyeth, P., & Purchase, H. C. (2002). Tangible programming elements for young children. In *CHI'02 extended abstracts on Human factors in computing systems* (pp. 774–775). ACM.

Design Principles

Programming Languages for Young Children

As a designer of playground experiences for coding, I need to understand the developmental characteristics of young children and the context in which they are likely to engage with programming.

Early childhood is a wonderful time in life. Four- to 7-year-old children are curious and eager to learn, but they get fatigued easily and have short attention spans. They learn better when engaged in doing things, and they like to talk. They are active and energetic, but they need frequent breaks and rest periods. While they tend to have developed gross motor skills, they are still working on fine motor skills, thus activities that engage small muscles can be difficult for them. They enjoy organized games and are concerned about following rules and fairness. They are imaginative and enjoy being involved in fantasy play. They tend to be competitive, self-assertive, and self-centered. They are learning how to cooperate with others and become team players. While they understand other people's feelings they might be unaware of how their own actions affect them. However, they are very sensitive to praise and recognition. Their feelings are easily hurt.

Children at this age tend to be inconsistent in their level of maturity and might behave one way at home and a different way at school; they might regress when tired and have a low level of tolerance for frustration. Academically speaking, there is a noticeable range of abilities: while some children might read, write, and be at ease with addition and subtraction, others are still working at recognizing letters and numbers. Given these developmental characteristics, designing programming languages for young children can be challenging.

Using the playground as a guiding metaphor is useful. It invites us to focus on the kinds of experiences we want children to have with technology and the kinds of interactions we want them to have with each other through coding.

The way we design can engage, encourage, and promote certain experiences while hindering others. For example, while programming with KIBO allows the use of materials such as recyclables and arts and crafts, programming with ScratchJr presents the opportunity to draw with computer tools. Tools have unique design features that enable different types of experiences. Experiences are powerful because they have an emotional impact (Brown, 2009). They transform us. They immerse us. They influence our worldviews. They engage us in action. When thinking about designing programming languages for children we must think first about the kinds of experiences we want them to have. Within the playground approach, we are concerned with promoting positive youth development, and not only with improving problem solving and mastering the art of coding.

In previous work (Bers, 2012), I presented several dimensions to guide the design of positive youth experiences in the digital landscape: developmental milestones, curriculum connections, technological infrastructure, mentoring model, diversity, communities of users, design process, access environment, and institutional context. The following paragraphs apply these to coding for young children.

Developmental Milestones

What are the developmental needs of young coders? What are their developmental challenges and milestones? What are the developmental conflicts they are most likely to encounter? Children accomplish different developmental tasks at different ages. Erikson (1950) described how each stage of development presents its own unique challenges, which he called "crises." Successful development of the personality (or psychosocial development) depends on meeting and overcoming these crises. The Ericksonian psychosocial framework proposes that at each stage the developing child, or adult, is confronted with a conflict of opposing forces.

Erikson described eight stages from infancy to adulthood (Erikson, 1950). All stages are present at birth but only begin to unfold according to both a natural scheme and one's ecological and cultural upbringing. In each stage, the person confronts, and hopefully masters, new challenges. Each stage builds upon the successful completion of earlier stages.

However, mastery of a stage is not required to advance to the next stage. The outcome of one stage is not permanent and can be modified by later experiences. Stages tend to be associated with life experiences and therefore with age. Erikson's stage theory characterizes an individual advancing through the eight life stages as a function of negotiating his or her biological and sociocultural forces.

How does Erickson's psychosocial theory influence the design of a programing language for young children? Let's look at ScratchJr and KIBO, designed for children between 4 and 7 years old, a range that includes two different Ericksonian life stages. On the one hand, children 4 to 5 years old are likely to traverse through the developmental crisis "initiative vs. guilt." The resolution, according to Erickson, comes when children develop a sense of purpose. On the other hand, children age 5 to 7 are engaged in "industry vs. inferiority" and solve it by gaining competence. The child must deal with the demands of learning new skills or risk feeling inferiority, failure, and incompetence. Programming languages need to reward and encourage purpose and competence. With this knowledge at hand, we designed both ScratchJr and KIBO so children could be challenged, but at the same time, master computer programming by making their own projects to share with others. Recognizing the importance of child-initiated activities, both environments can be used with minimum instruction. Both offer opportunities for challenges, and reward persistence and motivation. Design features accommodate different learning styles and developmental abilities in the continuum pre-operational to concrete cognitive stage development proposed by Piaget and followers (Case, 1984; Feldman, 2004; Fischer, 1980; Piaget, 1951; 1952). They also engage children with different preferences in terms of sensory skills and self-regulatory mechanisms. Children are challenged to achieve at a level just beyond their current mastery and have opportunities to practice newly acquired skills.

Curriculum Connections

How does coding facilitate or hinder the teaching of age-appropriate concepts and skills? How does it introduce ideas that children will encounter later, as they continue their educational journey? Sometimes learning computer programming is a goal itself; but most often, it is a way to learn about other things. For example, coding engages sequential and logical thinking, and this kind of thinking is also involved in literacy and math. When designing programming languages, it is wise to align interface design not only with the powerful ideas of computer science, but also with traditional school subjects. This strengthens curricular connections across disciplines.

For example, in ScratchJr we designed a grid that can be overlaid on the stage to help children understand the XY coordinates. While young children are not learning about the Cartesian system yet, it was important to us to have our software provide an experience that will later facilitate the understanding of those concepts. In KIBO we implemented sensors that take input from the environment. Most early childhood settings engage children in the study of their own five senses, so curricular connections can easily be made.

Technological Infrastructure

The digital landscape offers many technological platforms upon which to design computer programming languages for young children. For example, ScratchJr is an app that runs on tablets and computers; and KIBO is a stand-alone robotic kit that doesn't require another platform. As designers, it is important to understand the pros and cons of each platform and how they might have an impact on the usability of the tool. For example, while from a technological viewpoint it might have made sense to develop ScratchJr to work on a server and be accessible online, we discarded that option because most early childhood settings did not have reliable access to the internet in their preschool and kindergarten classes. With KIBO we experimented with incorporating the ability for users to 3D print their own sensor casings. We later decided against this because most teachers reported that they do not have access to 3D printers and lack the time to spend learning this process.

Mentoring Model

When developing programming languages for young children, we must think about how those young children will encounter the tool. Most likely, an adult, either in the home or school setting, will make the introduction. Once children first learn about it, how will they code on a recurring basis? Programming is a longitudinal activity. It is not something that we do once or in just "one hour of code." Those are wonderful introductory activities but, just like textual literacy doesn't develop in one hour, neither does computational literacy. Will children need an adult every time they want to code? Can they access the programming environment on their own? Thinking about the role that adults can play is important when designing for young children. What kind of expertise do adults need? Are the adults serving as coaches and mentors in the learning process, or are they playing the role of gatekeepers of the experience? Are they taking on a teaching role? What kind of training, if any, should they receive? In the case of ScratchJr, the app itself needs to be installed by an adult, but after that initial intervention, children can figure things out on their own by trial and error. But, to learn more sophisticated commands, they do need the help of an adult.

Young children might or might not read, so we decided to make all the icons self-explanatory. Adults told us they wanted instructions on the screen, so we chose to have words displayed when the user taps the icons. This design decision provides the needed scaffold for adults, without distracting the children. In the case of KIBO, an adult needs to show to the child for the first time how to scan the blocks. But, after that, there is only one button to press to make the robot move according to its program. Once the child learns how to scan and when to press the button, the child can use KIBO on his or her own.

Diversity

The term "diversity" usually makes us think about ethnic, racial, religious, and socioeconomic composition. However, in this context, the fundamental diversity question we want to ask is: what are the diverse experiences that children can have when coding? Can they have diversity in their approaches to making projects? Can they reach diversity of solutions? The richness of a programming language is in its potential to use it as a tool to create anything. Just like a paintbrush and a paint palette, a programming language must support children in expanding their imaginations. But, when giving a paint palette to young children, we do not overwhelm them with hundreds of colors. Similarly, when creating a programming language, we give them a manageable palette of programming commands. Both KIBO and ScratchJr have simple commands that, when combined, can produce powerful results. To the expert adult programmer, it might seem that some important ones, such as variables, are missing, but for a young child who is not familiar with the concept, that is not a problem. As children grow, they will be ready to move on to more sophisticated programming languages that have bigger and more complex programming palettes (for example, from ScratchJr to Scratch, or from KIBO to Lego robotics).

Program Scale

What is the size of the population we expect to use the programming language? Is there a need of a minimum critical mass to sustain participants' engagement (this tends to be the case when building a social network or a virtual community around the technology)? Is the language open source and, therefore, can others improve on it? If so, is that process going to be managed? How? In the case of both ScratchJr and KIBO we decided that, for now, we are aiming for users worldwide, but we would not invite developers to join us in working on the tools since we do not have the support mechanisms in place for a successful open source experience. With ScratchJr, we initiated a process of language localization not only for the app itself, which has already been translated into seven languages including English, but also for the associated curricular materials and book (Bers & Resnick, 2015), which has been translated to multiple languages. The ScratchJr team publishes a new version of the ScratchJr app every three to six months to add new languages. Meanwhile, the KIBO robot is being used in 48 states across the U.S., in public and private schools, as well as in home settings. Globally, KIBO (which is not as reliant on words and translations as ScratchJr) has been used in 43 countries and the number is steadily growing.

Communities of Users

Most programming languages, as they become successful, start to build a community of users. Some of these communities are virtual and others meet face to face. Some are active at developing support mechanisms for its members, and creating online tutorials, blogs, and YouTube channels, and others are more passive. In the case of programming languages for young children, the fundamental question is: who are the users that need to be part of the community? Is it the children themselves? Are the parents, teachers, or other adults involved? How many different communities need to be in place? And how are these managed? Depending on how we answer that question, different strategies need to be put in place.

With both ScratchJr and KIBO we have active mailing lists with thousands of users. While the ScratchJr mailing list sends information about news, app updates, and community events, the KIBO mailing list is a monthly newsletter that includes tips for learning KIBO's new modules, articles featuring teachers who are using KIBO in innovative ways, and curricular ideas. Furthermore, since both ScratchJr and KIBO are meant to be used by two communities at the same time (children and adults), we decided to launch a Family Days initiative that brings together children and their families to learn about coding and technology through collaborative activities.

Design Process

When designing any product, it is important to involve all potential users in the design process. In the case of programming languages for young children, parents, educators, and children need to be recruited in this effort. This might complicate things, as these are three distinct groups of users with different goals. However, these groups need to have their voices heard. Young children can't participate in online surveys and focus groups as adults can. In order to express their opinions and preferences, children need to have early access to prototypes. In the same way that they learn by doing, we learn by watching them. This poses some obvious challenges that can be mostly solved with low-tech prototypes and Wizard of Oz simulations. In the field of human–computer interaction, the Wizard of Oz technique is a research experiment in which subjects interact with a computer system that they believe to be autonomous, but which is actually being operated, or partially operated, by an unseen human being.

Teachers need to envision how they can integrate the programming language into their daily teaching routine; early studies with prototypes need to be conducted in classrooms and other settings where the programming language will be used. It is not enough to conduct pilot studies in the safety of the research lab. This iterative design process in which all stakeholders are involved is time consuming and expensive. For example, for both KIBO and ScratchJr we engaged in at least three years of research with early prototypes before releasing the products.

Access Environment

To use a programming language, we need access to it. Are young children able to have access on their own or do they need the help of teachers and parents? At school, the teacher might play the role of coordinator to have the needed technology available. But at home, things are different. For example, ScratchJr runs on a tablet. Do young children have access to it independently or do they need to use their parents' device? Are they competing for this resource with other family members? Many families only give young children a limited amount of "free choice" screen time each day. This means that children's access to programming apps like ScratchJr must compete with video games and television shows. Alternatively, the KIBO bin is easy for young children to open and close on their own and prompts children to take charge of cleaning up and putting away their own materials. However, robotics kits like KIBO may still raise similar access questions to ScratchJr. For example, do parents keep KIBO in their child's bedroom or playroom where they have free access to it, just like their other toys? Or do they treat it like their tablets and other "expensive technologies" and store it on a shelf that requires an adult's help to access? These questions of storage and access can change the way children experience the coding playground.

Institutional Context

What kind of financial model will make possible the design and later sustainability of the programming language? This question needs to be asked at an early stage. When a new product enters the educational market, teachers need to be trained, curriculum needs to be adjusted, new materials need to be bought, etc. These changes shouldn't happen if there is no assurance that the new environment will be "alive" and supported for as long as it is needed. Designing a programming language for young children is a major endeavor. Similarly, financial sustainability is essential not only to launch the program, but also to update it and fix bugs. It is important to be aware of this before embarking on a project that might be well thought out and of excellent quality, but cannot pay the bills. Both in the case of ScratchJr and KIBO, we received generous funding from the National Science Foundation to initiate the projects. Now, the Scratch Foundation provides the needed financial support to continue the work on ScratchJr, allowing us to keep it as a free app; while KinderLab Robotics, through a competitive NSF SBIR grant for small business, angel funding, and revenues from sales, can commercialize KIBO worldwide.

While the dimensions presented in this chapter do not focus on specific technological features, they provide a wider lens to understand the richness of the context in which the technology will be used. However, although it is important to design developmentally appropriate tools for early education, it is also important to understand that the learning of coding and the development of computational thinking happen in the context of an overall curricular experience. The next chapter will focus on teaching strategies for making a coding playground.

References

Bers, M. U. (2012). *Designing digital experiences for positive youth development: From playpen to playground.* Cary, NC: Oxford.

Bers, M.U. & Resnick, M. (2015). *The Official ScratchJr Book.* San Francisco, CA: No Starch Press.

Brown, T. (2009). *Change by design: How design thinking transforms organizations and inspires innovation.* New York: Harper Collins.

Case, R. (1984). The process of stage transition: A neo-Piagetian view. In R. Sternberg (Ed.), *Mechanisms of cognitive development* (pp. 19–44). San Francisco, CA: Freeman.

Erikson, E. H. (1950). *Childhood and society.* New York: Norton.

Feldman, D. H. (2004). Piaget's stages: The unfinished symphony of cognitive development. *New Ideas in Psychology, 22*, 175–231. doi: 10.1016/j.newideapsych.2004.11.005

Fischer, K. W. (1980). A theory of cognitive development: The control and construction of hierarchies of skills. *Psychological review, 87*(6), 477–531.

Gmitrova, V., & Gmitrova, J. (2004). The primacy of child-directed pretend play on cognitive competence in a mixed-age environment: Possible interpretations. *Early Child Development and Care, 174*(3), 267–279.

Leseman, P. P., Rollenberg, L., & Rispens, J. (2001). Playing and working in kindergarten: Cognitive co-construction in two educational situations. *Early Childhood Research Quarterly, 16*(3), 363–384.

Piaget, J. (1951). Egocentric thought and sociocentric thought. *J. Piaget, Sociological Studies*, 270–286.

Piaget, J. (1952). *The origins of intelligence in children* (Vol. 8, No. 5, pp. 18–1952). New York: International Universities Press.

Scarlett, W. G., Naudeau, S., Ponte, I., & Salonius-Pasternak, D. (2005). *Children's play*. Thousand Oaks, CA: Sage.

Vygotsky, L. (1976). Play and its role in the mental development of the child. In J. Bruner, A. Jolly, & K. Sylva (Eds.), *Play: Its role in development and evolution*. New York: Basic Books.

Teaching Strategies

12
Coding in the Early Curriculum

In my previous life, before coming to the U.S. for graduate school, I worked as a journalist. As such, I learned to ask five questions: what, why, where, when, and how. Now, as we are nearing the end of the book, I will address each of these questions. The "what" is the core of this manuscript: coding, and the associated powerful ideas from the domain of computer science. The "why" has been answered throughout this book, but especially in the chapters of Part I when we explored the cognitive, personal, social, and emotional dimensions of coding. The "where" and "when" receive different answers according to the particular context and setting in which young children code: home, school, an after-school program, the library, a makerspace, etc. The chapters on ScratchJr and KIBO provided some examples. Finally, the "how" is the overall approach and my contribution to this growing field: a playground approach to coding grounded on the PTD theoretical framework.

As teachers, theoretical frameworks are useful for providing guiding principles for designing, implementing, and evaluating curricular experiences. This chapter shares teaching strategies that I have found helpful over the years when introducing young children to coding.

Teaching can be defined as creating the needed conditions for children to encounter and explore powerful ideas. Let's go back to Seymour Papert's book, *Mindstorms: Children, Computers and Powerful Ideas*. He used to regret that readers of his book thought the key concepts were children and computers. In his perspective, the book was about powerful ideas. Powerful ideas is one of the most complex concepts to understand within Papert's Constructionist approach to education and probably one of the most intellectually rewarding.

The potential of computers for education lies in their power to engage children in encountering powerful ideas. Thus, curriculum should be built around powerful ideas. In this book, Chapter 6 explores the powerful ideas of computer science that young children encounter while coding. Throughout this book, and specifically in Chapters 2 and 3 of Part II, we learned about these powerful ideas and how they engage children in computational thinking.

Over the years, a growing community of researchers and educators has used the term "powerful ideas" to refer to a set of intellectual tools worth learning, as decided by a community of experts in each of the fields of study (Bers, 2008). However, different people have used the term in diverse ways and amongst the powerful ideas community there are divergent opinions about the benefits and dangers of presenting a unified definition (Papert & Resnick, 1996).

Papert's Constructionism is about powerful ideas. He envisioned the computer as a carrier of new and old powerful ideas and as an agent for educational change. While school reform is a complex topic, Constructionism contributes to this dialogue by proposing the introduction of coding in the classroom as a way to restructure learning and to encounter powerful ideas.

The importance paid by Papert and colleagues to the world of ideas and thinking derives from the Piagetian legacy concerned with epistemology: understanding how we know what we know, how we construct knowledge, and how we think. Thinking is at the core of why we introduce coding in early childhood. Coding helps children think in systematic and sequential ways.

This book shows how thinking can happen in a playful way. The statue "The Thinker," by Auguste Rodin, which shows a male figure sitting on a rock with his chin resting on one hand as though deep in thought, is often used to represent thinking as a stationary and passive activity. However, research shows that thinking is embodied and happens as we engage in all kind of activities, including playing (Hutchins, 1995; Kiefer & Trumpp, 2012; Wilson & Foglia, 2011). When coding, children think about algorithms, modularity, control structures, representation, the design process, debugging, hardware, and software, but they also think about their own thinking.

Powerful ideas are intellectual tools. They evoke an emotional response. Children can make connections between powerful ideas and personal interests, passions and past experiences. Early childhood education has paid particular attention to promoting learning environments in which children can make connections. Emergent curriculum builds upon children's interests and is responsive to the ideas, excitement, and questions from the children themselves (Rinaldi, 1998). NAEYC guidelines for promoting integrated curricula are close in spirit to the Constructionist notion of powerful ideas. These guidelines call for powerful principles or concepts applied generally across disciplines (i.e., that support the development of new ideas and concepts) and emerging from and connecting to children's personal interests (Bredekamp & Rosegrant, 1995).

How Do We Think About a Coding Curriculum?

Curriculum facilitates the encounter with powerful ideas in a connected and developmentally appropriate way. It is helpful to think about the following considerations when the goal of the curriculum is to promote computational thinking through playful coding.

1. **Pacing:** It's important to consider the scope and sequence of activities designed to engage with the powerful ideas of computer science. The curriculum can be designed to happen over the course of one intensive week of coding, over the course of a few months with one or two sessions per week, or over the course of a year.

2. **Types of coding activities:** Some are structured challenges, while others involve free exploration. While structured challenges convey powerful ideas in a modular format and ensure that every child participating in the experience will be exposed to the same materials, free exploration provides opportunities for playing with ideas and discovering things independently. Allocating time for free exploration helps build a solid foundation.

3. **Materials:** To code we need tools. Although computational thinking can be explored through low-tech materials such as printed icons of the different programming commands of a programming language, this is no substitution for the programming language itself. Accessibility to the materials is important. For example, when working with robots, some teachers may choose to give a complete robotic kit to each group

of students. Children may label the kit with their name(s) and use the same kit for the duration of the curriculum. Other teachers may choose to take apart the kits and have materials sorted by type and place all the materials in a central location for children to choose as needed. If working with tablets, it is important to remind children that they need to be charged. Some schools provide carts that roll the tablets into the classroom and therefore children and teachers do not need to worry about batteries running out. Other classrooms have their own equipment, and it is therefore the teacher's responsibility to have everything ready to use. Regardless of the technological platform, it is crucial to set expectations for how to use and treat materials. These issues are important not only in making the curriculum logistically easier to implement, but also because, as described in the Reggio Emilia tradition, the environment can act as the "third teacher" (Darragh, 2006).

4. **Classroom management:** Teaching in an early childhood setting requires careful planning and ongoing adjustments when it comes to classroom management. This may play out differently during technology-rich activities because of the novelty of the materials themselves. It is important to provide a clear structure and set of expectations for using the materials and for the routines of each part of the lessons (e.g., technology circles, clean up time, etc.).

5. **Group sizes:** As in any other kind of early childhood initiative, the experience can be whole group, small group, in pairs, or individual. Whether individual work is feasible depends on the availability of materials, which may be limited. However, an effort should be made to allow students to work in as small a group as is possible. Some classes structure technology time to fit into a "center time" in the schedule, in which students rotate through small stations around the room with different activities at each location. This format gives students more access to teachers when they have questions and lets teachers tailor instruction and feedback as well as assess each student's progress more easily than during whole-group work. Working in small groups is not similar to doing individual work. Let's use a comparison from literacy. When learning how to write, children do not share their pens. Each child has a pen and can spend as much time as needed struggling with it. While

group work promotes conversation, multiple voices, and viewpoints, it's still important to make time for individual work.

6. **Addressing state and national frameworks**: At the time of writing this book, there are no national frameworks in the U.S. that address computational thinking and coding in the early years. Many initiatives are on their way (e.g., Code.org, Computing Leaders ACM, & CSTA, 2016; U.S. Department of Education & Office of Innovation and Improvement, 2016), and several countries have already made coding mandatory. However, some of the powerful ideas involved in computational thinking are foundational for other academic subjects, such as math, literacy, engineering, and science. Additionally, coding provides a powerful way to integrate disciplinary knowledge and skills. Thus, it is useful to make a deliberate planning effort to map how each of the powerful ideas from coding relates to traditional disciplinary content knowledge and skills mandated by federal and state frameworks.

7. **Assessments:** With the playground approach to coding, children certainly have fun; however, evaluating the learning process and the learning outcomes is important. There are many ways to do this: documenting student's projects and ways of talking about and sharing their projects; analyzing their design journals where they keep different iterations of a same project; completing worksheets aimed at testing specific knowledge; collecting work portfolios; using assessment instruments such as the Solve-Its tasks and "Engineering licenses" developed by my DevTech research group (Strawhacker & Bers, 2015). These tools can serve to evaluate individual children's learning, while they are working in groups (DevTech, 2015).

Before bringing coding into the early classroom, teachers will find it helpful to think about the seven conditions presented above. A curriculum of powerful ideas from computer science can be conveyed with different pedagogical approaches. This book presents the playground approach to coding, which is grounded on the PTD framework (Bers, 2012) and the 6 Cs or positive behaviors that can be found both in the playground and the coding class: creation, creativity, communication, collaboration, community building, and choices of conduct. Let's review them (see Figure 12.1).

Positive Technological Development (PTD) framework

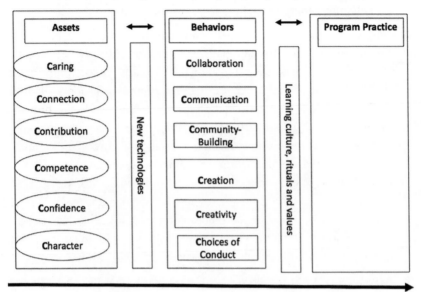

Personal development trajectory within a socio cultural context

Figure 12.1 The PTD framework developed by Bers (2012). PTD proposes six positive behaviors (6 C's) that should be supported by educational programs that use new educational technologies. These are: creation, creativity, communication, collaboration, community building, and choices of conduct. The third column, Program Practice, is left blank for educators to complete on their own based on their own classroom cultures, practices, and rituals.

1. ***Content creation***, by making a project and programming it. The design process and the computational thinking involved in programming foster *competence* in computer literacy and technological fluency.

2. ***Creativity***, by fostering opportunities for children to develop their own project ideas, as opposed to copying them from a booklet or following instructions, and by providing different materials for children to work with. As children approach solving technical problems in creative ways, they develop a sense of *confidence* in their learning potential.

3. ***Collaboration***, by engaging children in a learning environment that promotes working in teams, sharing resources, and *caring* about each other. Collaboration is defined here as getting or giving help with a

project, programming together, lending or borrowing materials, or working together on a common task.

4. **Communication**, through mechanisms that promote a sense of *connection* between peers or with adults, such as technology circles. Technology circles present a good opportunity for problem solving as a community. To cover all the important ideas without losing the children's attention, the discussions might be broken up and held throughout the day rather than all at once. It can also be helpful to make a "Robot or Tablet Parking Lot" for the materials while they are not in use so children can focus at the technology circles.

5. **Community building**, through scaffolded opportunities to form a learning community that promotes the *contribution* of ideas. Our long-term educational goal is not only to foster computational thinking and technological fluency amongst the participating children and teachers, but also amongst the wider community. Open houses provide authentic opportunities for children to share and celebrate the learning process and tangible products with others who are also invested in their learning. During these open houses, family, friends, and community members visit the class for a demonstration of the children's final projects. Each child is given the opportunity not only to run their robot or project on a tablet or computer, but to also play the role of teacher as they explain how they built, programmed, and worked through problems.

6. **Choices of conduct**, which provide children with the opportunity to experiment with "what if" questions and potential consequences, and to provoke examination of values and exploration of *character traits*. Taking care of materials, respecting rules about technology use, and differentiation of roles are important to the growth of a responsible learning community. Teachers may assign children "expertise badges" that carry the responsibility of helping others on a topic for which the child is an expert, and at the same time, encourage the child to try on new roles and be flexible. The focus on learning to code is as important as helping children develop an inner compass to guide their actions in a just and responsible way. Choices of conduct are not only made by children. Teachers also make important choices in the way they display and introduce the materials to the children.

Developmentally appropriate programming languages are crucial for introducing coding in early childhood education. Furthermore, in this book I show how these environments are best suited when designed with a "coding as literacy" approach, as opposed to a "coding as problem solving" approach. This means that children can easily develop fluency with the language to become producers of their own computational projects to share with others. In the process of programming, they solve many problems, but the educational goal is beyond problem solving. The goal is personal expression and communication.

When young children are learning to read and write, we provide them with different kinds of books and different types of writing materials that are developmentally appropriate. Diversity enriches their literacy experience; likewise, this is true with coding tools. Being able to fluently use ScratchJr, KIBO, and any of the other programming languages described earlier enriches their computational thinking.

Educators who want to introduce coding in the early childhood classroom need these programming languages, but they also need a curriculum of the powerful ideas of computer science that is developmentally appropriate and a guiding framework that understands the whole child. I have proposed the PTD framework and its six positive behaviors as a framework that integrates cognitive, personal, social, emotional, and moral dimensions of early childhood. Armed with the programming languages, the curriculum and the framework, the early childhood educator can venture into the fun of a coding playground.

References

Bers, M. (2008). *Blocks to robots: Learning with technology in the early childhood classroom.* New York, NY: Teachers College Press.

Bers, M. U. (2012). *Designing digital experiences for positive youth development: From playpen to playground.* Cary, NC: Oxford.

Bredekamp, S., & Rosegrant, T., eds. (1995). *Reaching potentials: Transforming early childhood curriculum and assessment* (Vol. 2). Washington, DC: NAEYC.

Code.org, Computing Leaders ACM, and CSTA. (2016). Announcing a new framework to define K-12 computer science education [Press release]. *Code.org.* Retrieved from https://code.org/framework-announcement

Darragh, J. C. (2006). *The environment as the third teacher.* Retrieved from www.eric.ed.gov/PDFS/ED493517.pdf

DevTech Research Group. (2015). *Sample engineer's license.* Retrieved from http://api.ning.com/files/HFuYSlzj6Lmy18EzB9-sGv4ftGAZpfkGS fCe6lHFFQmv8PaelQB-4PB8kS6BunpzNhbtYhqnlmEWpFBwQJdfH7y FrJrgUUrl/BlankEngineerLicense.jpg

Hutchins, E. (1995). *Cognition in the Wild.* Cambridge, MA: MIT Press.

Kiefer, M., & Trumpp, N. M. (2012). Embodiment theory and education: The foundations of cognition in perception and action. *Trends in Neuroscience and Education, 1*(1), 15–20.

Papert, S. (1980). *Mindstorms: Children, computers, and powerful ideas.* New York: Basic Books, Inc.

Papert, S. (2000). What's the big idea? Toward a pedagogy of idea power. *IBM Systems Journal, 39*(3–4), 720–729.

Papert, S., & Resnick, M. (1996). *Paper presented at Rescuing the Powerful Ideas, an NSF-sponsored symposium at MIT,* Cambridge, MA.

Rinaldi, C. (1998). Projected curriculum constructed through documentation—Progettazione: An interview with Lella Gandini. In C. Edwards, L. Gandini, & G. Forman (Eds.), *The hundred languages of children: The Reggio Emilia approach—Advanced reflections* (2nd ed., pp. 113–125). Greenwich, CT: Ablex.

Strawhacker, A. L., & Bers, M. U. (2015). "I want my robot to look for food": Comparing children's programming comprehension using tangible, graphical, and hybrid user interfaces. *International Journal of Technology and Design Education, 25*(3), 293–319.

U.S. Department of Education, & Office of Innovation and Improvement. (2016). *STEM 2026: A vision for innovation in STEM education.* Washington, DC: Author.

Wilson, R. A., & Foglia, L. (2011). Embodied cognition. *Stanford Encyclopedia of Philosophy.*

Conclusion

It is 3 p.m. on a sunny Monday and I just finished giving a talk for hundreds of early childhood teachers in the Boston area. As I am making my way out of the room, a shy woman approaches me. She wants to know if she should allow her 6-year-old to use ScratchJr on her own and how often. I smile at her. I have heard this question many times. I ask her, "Will you allow her to read a book? How often? Will you allow her to write a story? How many of them? Always?" She replies: "It depends. It depends what book and it depends when she wants to write. I will not let her write a story while we are having a family dinner, and I certainly do not let her read some grown-up books I have at home. They can be scary for her." In order to answer my question, this woman carefully considered the context. Similar logic applies to the use of technology: it depends.

Coding is a playground. It offers many opportunities for learning and personal growth, exploration and creativity, mastery of new skills, and ways of thinking. We do not always take children to the playground. There are other places to visit and other skills to develop. But when we do go to the playground, we want it to be a developmentally appropriate space.

This book explores the role of coding in early childhood. It draws on the framework of Positive Technological Development (PTD) to understand the developmental milestones and playful learning experiences that children can have while developing computational thinking and exploring powerful ideas from computer science. Furthermore, it proposes that coding can be a playground for children to become producers, and not merely consumers, in our technologically rich world.

The playground approach to coding that I present moves the conversation beyond the traditional view of coding as a technical skill. Coding is a literacy. As such, it invites new ways of thinking and carries the ability to produce an artifact detached from its creator, with its own meaning. There is a producer with an intention, with a passion, with a desire to communicate something. Coding, like writing, is a medium of human expression. Through this expressive process, we learn to think, feel, and communicate in new ways. This book takes a stance against problem solving as the primary goal of teaching young children to code. Instead, I propose coding to support fluent personal expression.

In the coding playground, young children create their own projects to communicate ideas and express who they are. They need developmentally appropriate tools, like KIBO and ScratchJr. They engage in problem solving and storytelling; they develop sequencing skills and algorithmic thinking. They journey through the design process from an early idea to a final product that can be shared with others. They learn how to manage frustration and find a solution, rather than giving up when things get challenging. They develop strategies for debugging their projects. They learn to collaborate with others and they grow proud of their hard work. In the coding playground, children have fun while learning new things. They can be themselves and playfully explore new concepts and ideas, as well as develop new skills. They can fail and start all over again.

In this coding playground, children encounter powerful ideas from computer science that are useful not only for future programmers and engineers, but for everyone. Coding is a way to achieve literacy in the twenty-first century, like reading and writing. It needs to start early. Today, those who can produce digital technologies, and not only consume them, will be in charge of their own destiny. Literacy is a medium of human power. Those who know how to read and write can assert their voices. Those who do not are disenfranchised. Will this be true for those who cannot code? For those who cannot think computationally?

It is our responsibility to introduce children to coding and computational thinking when they are young. We know that, as a literacy, coding will open doors, many of them that we cannot anticipate now. But we also know that these young coders are still children. As such, they deserve the best we can give them. It is not enough to copy models of computer science education developed for elementary or high school students. It is not good to give them programming languages created for older children, which are not developmentally appropriate for them.

As teachers, we need technologies and curriculum specifically designed for young children that take into consideration their cognitive,

social, and emotional needs. This is novel territory. Therefore, these children are our best collaborators, as they can guide us through the complexity of their thinking. As researchers, we need to explore the developmental
stages of learning to code and the learning trajectories associated with
computational thinking. We must understand what is truly happening
when a 4-year-old programs her robot to dance the Hokey Pokey, and
a 5-year-old makes an animation. While there is a growing movement
towards STEAM education and research methodologies from those disciplines, we also look at research on literacy to elucidate some of these
learning processes. Coding can be studied not only as a problem-solving
mechanism, but as a process that allows the creation of a shareable product of human expression.

As teachers all over the world begin to incorporate coding and computational thinking in early childhood education, may we have the clarity
to understand how these can be integrated into pre-existing early childhood educational practices. May we see the children in their totality, as
individuals with their own voices and their own stories to tell, and not only
as problem solvers. May we encourage and support their playfulness as a
way of learning.